THE MILITIA MOVEMENT IN AMERICA

Before and After Oklahoma City

THE MILITIA MOVEMENT IN AMERICA

Before and After Oklahoma City

TRICIA ANDRYSZEWSKI

The Millbrook Press
Brookfield, Connecticut

Photographs courtesy of Corbis-Bettmann: pp. 11, 17, 21, 24, 61, 76;
Impact Visuals: pp. 30 (© 1989 Lonny Shavelson), 34 (© Donna Binder),
36 (© Jim West), 41 (© Kirk Condyles), 49 (© 1995 Jay Mallin), 71 (©
Donna Binder), 75 (© Jim West), 107 (© 1996 Paul Dix); AP/Wide World
Photos: pp. 50, 55, 66, 85, 94, 112.

Library of Congress Cataloging-in-Publication Data
Andryszewski, Tricia, 1956–
The militia movement in America : before and after Oklahoma City /
Tricia Andryszewski.
p. cm.
Summary: Explores the roots of the militia movement's growth in the
United States, its connection with mainstream society, the ideologies of
anti-government groups, and the tragedies at Ruby Ridge, Waco, and
Oklahoma City.
ISBN 0-7613-0119-4
1. Militia movements—United States—Juvenile literature. 2. Terrorism—
United States—Juvenile literature. 3. Political crimes and offenses—United
States—Juvenile literature. 4. United States—Social conditions—Juvenile
literature. 5. United States—Politics and government—Juvenile literature.
[1. Militia movements. 2. Government, resistance to. 3. Terrorism. 4.
Political crimes and offenses. 5. United States—Social conditions. 6.
United States—Politics and government.] I. Title.
HV6432.A55 1997   320.4'2'0973—dc20   96-32178   CIP   AC

Published by The Millbrook Press, Inc., Brookfield, Connecticut

CONTENTS

THE MILITIA MOVEMENT IN AMERICA

Before and After Oklahoma City

PROLOGUE
April 19, 1995

Just after 9 A.M. on Wednesday, April 19, 1995, the Alfred
P. Murrah Federal Building in downtown Oklahoma City
was settling into its usual workday routine. More than
500 government workers, employees of federal agencies
including the Social Security Administration, Housing and
Urban Development, Veterans Affairs, the Marines, the
Secret Service, the Drug Enforcement Administration,
and the Bureau of Alcohol, Tobacco and Firearms, shared
the nine-story concrete-and-steel office building. So did
about thirty children, mostly children of workers in the
building, who spent their days at a day-care center on the
second floor. Dozens of people who didn't work for the
government—from delivery workers to retirees visiting
the Social Security office—were also in the building at
the time.

Then, at 9:02 A.M., an explosion ripped off the north
face of the building. The force of the blast actually tilted
the building into the air. As each floor landed it "pan-
caked" with the floor below it, stacking up in a dense
heap of rubble two stories high that sprawled clear across

the street. Cars near the building burst into flames. Windows were broken and office workers were thrown from their chairs blocks away from the explosion, which was felt as far as 30 miles (48 kilometers) away.

Moments later, survivors began to stagger out of the building, many of them bleeding badly. But they, at least, had survived. The force of the explosion had literally blown other victims apart, and even propelled bodies through the cinderblock walls of the Social Security office.

A swarm of police, firefighters, and other rescue workers converged at the site. Looking for trapped survivors, they picked carefully through the debris—shattered concrete, twisted metal, broken office furniture, and children's toys.

Everyone at the site was haunted by the thought of the children whose day-care center was so close to the center of the explosion. How many children had been at the center that day, having breakfast, at 9:02 A.M.? How many had died? How many in the shattered building might be trapped, scared and injured?

"A whole floor," one firefighter said. "A whole floor of innocents. Grownups, you know, deserve a lot of the stuff they get. But why the children? What did the children ever do to anybody?" [1]

"The building is in danger of collapse," Assistant Fire Chief John Hansen said as the rescue workers pressed on. "We're talking to victims. We've got listening devices and dogs. But it's slow. We reach through cracks and hold people's hands and reassure them as we can. The firefighters are coming out with tears in their eyes." [2]

Dozens of dead and injured men, women, and children were carried out as the day wore on. Nearby hospi-

Searching for victims, rescue crews remove debris from the bombed-out facade of the Alfred P. Murrah Federal Building in Oklahoma City, which was destroyed by a truck bomb on April 19, 1995.

tals were overwhelmed. Frantic relatives and friends searched for hundreds of loved ones whose fates remained unknown long hours after the blast. A team of doctors amputated the crushed right leg of an injured young woman to free her from the rubble. About 10 P.M., a fifteen-year-old girl named Brandy was freed from the wreckage. She was the last victim to emerge from the building alive.

By that time, the search was well under way for the person or persons responsible for the explosion. Federal investigators very quickly concluded that the blast had been no accident. Someone had driven a car or a truck up to the building and left it there with hundreds, maybe thousands, of pounds of explosives packed inside. While rescuers searched for survivors, investigators combed the site looking for clues about the bomb: What was it made of? How was it constructed? Who left it there? Why?

In the early hours of the investigation, there was much speculation about whether the bomb might have been left by Middle Eastern terrorists, like the perpetrators of the 1993 bombing of the World Trade Center in New York City. Soon, however, attention focused on two suspects who weren't foreigners. From blasted bits found at the bomb site, investigators identified a rented truck that they believed had carried the explosives. On Thursday, the Federal Bureau of Investigation (FBI) released sketches and descriptions of two suspects wanted for arrest in the case—men apparently young, white, and American—who had rented the truck on Monday afternoon using false identification.

Meanwhile, the rescue effort continued. Exhausted workers slowly, painstakingly picked through tons of debris, taking great care not to endanger one another or anyone who might remain trapped beneath the heavy chunks of precariously piled concrete. By the end of the day on Thursday, 53 were confirmed dead and about 200 remained missing. No one had been taken out of the building alive since Wednesday night, and hopes of finding any more survivors were fading.

On Friday, Timothy McVeigh, one of the suspects wanted in connection with the rented truck, was taken into court and charged in the bombing. Two friends of McVeigh, Terry Nichols and his brother James Nichols, were questioned by investigators. The three were linked not to Middle Eastern terrorism, but to homegrown American "militias"—armed groups of antigovernment extremists.

By the weekend, the death toll in the bombing had risen to 78, with more than 400 injured and about 150 still missing.

President Bill Clinton declared Sunday a national day of mourning. That afternoon he addressed a memorial service in Oklahoma City attended by some 12,000 family members, friends, rescuers, coworkers, and neighbors of those hurt or killed in the bombing. "Today our nation joins with you in grief," he said. "We mourn with you. We share your hope against hope that some may still survive. We thank all those who have worked so heroically to save lives and to solve this crime. . . . We pledge to do all we can to help you heal the injured, to rebuild this city and to bring to justice those who did this evil." [3]

The following weekend, Governor Frank Keating of Oklahoma announced that workers at the bomb site had given up hope of finding any more survivors. Hundreds of rescue workers, who had come from all over the country to lend emergency assistance, at last headed home. Heavy machinery was brought in to move the remaining piles of rubble more quickly in a final search for bodies.

On May 4, late in the evening, the search was officially called off amid fears that the bombed-out remains of the building might collapse and kill rescue workers. On May 23, demolition experts imploded the parts of the building that were still standing, collapsing the dangerously unstable structure—by then an ugly, terrifying, nationally known landmark—into a heap of trash to be cleared away.

The final death toll from the bombing—the most deadly terrorist attack in U.S. history—was 168, including 1 rescue worker and 19 children.

As the initial shock of the bombing wore off, Americans across the country wondered how such a terrible thing could have happened. If Oklahoma City, in America's heartland, wasn't safe from terrorist attack, where was it safe? Equally disturbing, this bombing wasn't part of some foreign dispute brought into the United States by outsiders. Instead, the motivation of the bombing suspects seemed to have grown out of an entirely American climate of hatred and violence.

This book examines the roots of that climate of hatred and violence, its connection with mainstream American society, its flourishing in the militia movement of the 1990s, and its role in the Oklahoma City bombing and its aftermath.

CHAPTER ONE

An American Tradition of Hatred

"We must secure the existence of our people and a future for White children."

> "Fourteen Words" motto
> of David Lane, Order member
> convicted of hate crimes [1]

The militia movement (sometimes called the "patriot" movement) is an informal network of paramilitary activists, seeking to defend American citizens against what the activists see as threats to freedom, chiefly from the federal goverment.

The militia movement of the 1990s wasn't invented and created overnight. It grew out of a long tradition of hatred in America. The extremist ideas, organizations, and individuals that have inspired and shaped the militia movement include:

THE KU KLUX KLAN

The oldest and best-known hate movement in the United States, the Ku Klux Klan (KKK), began more than a century ago in the South after the Civil War. Klansmen wrapped in sheets, with hoods hiding their faces, threatened, harassed, robbed, assaulted, mutilated, raped, and murdered Southern blacks and destroyed their property. Their intention was to assert white supremacy, claiming that whites were the rightful rulers of America, and to terrorize the black population into submission.

In the early years of the twentieth century, after World War I, the Klan rose again. This time, however, its reach extended well beyond the Deep South to much of the rural Midwest and West. It pursued an aggressive political agenda, helping to elect mayors, governors, and congressmen sympathetic to the KKK's point of view. And, true to its roots, it also unleashed a wave of terrorist violence, not only against blacks but also against Jews, Catholics, "foreigners," and white women who exhibited too much independence. (The Klan even opposed allowing women the right to vote.)

In the late 1950s and early 1960s, Southern blacks and their supporters rose up and demanded full equality of opportunity for America's black citizens and an end to racial segregation. Many whites opposed this civil rights movement, and a revived Ku Klux Klan was able to recruit thousands of members to fight it. Klan actions ranged from beating up peaceful protesters (often with the tacit approval of local police) to lynchings. But the Klan failed to derail the civil rights movement.

In the 1970s several polished, media-savvy Klan leaders (most notably David Duke) managed to create for themselves an image of calm respectability and, with this image, to extend the Klan's reach into the American mainstream. (The American mainstream includes those ideas

The white supremacist hate movement known as the Ku Klux Klan, which originated in the South after the Civil War, is one of the historical antecedents of the militia movement of the 90s.

and institutions that most Americans feel comfortable with.) The new, media-friendly face of the Klan did not, however, replace the traditional hooded Klan activities. It also did not inspire a new mass following. Instead, by the end of the 1970s, the Klan was beginning to be what it is today—only a relatively small, though influential, element in a much bigger, complex, interconnected pattern of white supremacists and related hate groups and ideologies.

CHRISTIAN IDENTITY

Christian Identity is a quasi-religious white supremacist ideology. Although there are many Identity churches scattered around the country, Christian Identity also has been adopted in whole or in part by many white supremacists with no formal church ties, from Klan members to neo-Nazis to racist skinheads to militia members. (Among the reading materials that Oklahoma City bombing suspect Timothy McVeigh gave to his sister, Jennifer, was the Christian Identity newsletter *Patriot Report*.)

Christian Identity holds that the Bible is God's "direct communication with ONE special group of people: Israel, the descendants of Israel.... We affirm that the Anglo-Saxon, Celtic and kindred white peoples of the world are the direct descendants of Abraham, not the Jews as commonly believed throughout most of Christendom."[2] According to Christian Identity, not only are the Jewish people not "Israel" (the biblical "chosen people") but they are actually children of Satan, descended from a child fathered by Satan with Eve, the biblical first woman. The nonwhite, non-Jewish peoples of the world are considered "mud people," the spiritual equivalent of animals.

With this central belief always in mind, Christian Identity thoroughly reinterprets the Bible. The result is a relentlessly racist worldview justified by references to scripture.

The Identity interpretation of scripture also asserts that the great biblical battle between good and evil, Armageddon, is nearly upon us in the form of a worldwide race war. It is considered a sacred obligation for Identity believers to prepare for this race war, which, they believe, God has ordained only whites will survive.

Some Identity believers, who call themselves "survivalists," have acted on their beliefs by living apart from the rest of the world, in isolated communes or family farms, devoting themselves to preparing for the inevitable race war by acquiring stores of food, weapons and ammunition, and knowledge of wilderness survival techniques. According to James Ellison, former leader of the Covenant, Sword, and Arm of the Lord, a communal, Identity-oriented survivalist group active in the 1980s, "There will be an economic collapse, riots in the cities, famine, and war. People will kill each other for food, weapons, shelter, clothing, anything. It will get so bad that parents will eat their children."[3]

Perhaps the best-known Identity believer and survivalist has been Randy Weaver, whose face-off against federal agents at his home atop Ruby Ridge, Idaho, in August 1992, became a rallying symbol for antigovernment militias in the mid-1990s.

WHITE SEPARATISM

Many white supremacists believe in "white separatism" (also known as "white nationalism"). They favor the creation of an all-white nation, from which blacks, Jews, and other minorities would be banned. White separatists differ among themselves about where the boundaries of this white homeland should be drawn. Some prefer the already mostly white Northwest, others favor the old Confederate South, and still others would include all of North America. Any of these ideas for an all-white nation would involve considerable ethnic and racial cleansing—the forced removal of all nonwhite residents.

ANTI-AMERICAN
CONSPIRACY THEORIES

Since American colonial times, a long succession of conspirators have been accused of anti-American plots.[4] The most widely held American version of conspiracy theory in this century has been the anti-Communist version of the Cold War era. (Senator Joseph McCarthy built his career in the 1950s on accusations that Communists had infiltrated the highest levels of U.S. government, and that secret Communist agents were active throughout the United States in all walks of life.) More recently, in popular culture, conspiracy theories about the assassination of President John F. Kennedy have been perennial bestsellers.

For generations, most hate groups in America have subscribed to some variation of a conspiracy theory holding that a hidden elite, dominated by Jews, controls much of the world's real power. The conspiracy theory favored by the militia movement in the 1990s has retained this anti-Jewish element while emphasizing the dangers of a "New World Order" with one world government. According to this theory, the U.S. federal government has

Senator Joseph McCarthy testifying at a hearing on June 9, 1950, that an organized network of Communists had infiltrated all aspects of society throughout the United States.

become the dupe of the United Nations or of some secret internationalist cabal bent on enslaving Americans and dominating the entire world. Part of this agenda, white racialists typically believe, is the destruction of the white race through interbreeding with other races.

MINUTEMEN

In the 1960s, diverse right-wing extremists—Nazis, Klan members, Identity believers, and others—organized themselves to fight a Communist-dominated version of this conspiracy to take over the United States. Calling themselves "Minutemen" (after the Revolutionary War heroes), they formed small, secret cells with 5 to 15 members each. They armed themselves extensively and undertook paramilitary training to prepare themselves for the allegedly impending takeover attempt.

Although the Minutemen faded away in the early 1970s after the arrest of their leader, Robert DePugh, their example has remained an influential model for many hate groups. Their emphasis on paramilitary training was taken up by various groups of white supremacists beginning in the early 1980s. In the 1990s the militia movement emulated them as well.

NEO-NAZIS

Before World War II, Adolf Hitler attracted a small number of followers (including some Klansmen) in the United States. During and after the war, however, Hitler and his program of National Socialism (Nazism) were overwhelmingly unpopular in the United States. (National Socialism preaches that "Aryans," white northern Europeans and their descendants, are the world's master race, superior to all other peoples.) By the 1970s, however, wartime memories had faded, and some members of a new generation of white supremacists, known as neo-Nazis, began to look upon Hitler as a hero.

Banding together into such small parties as the National Socialist Party of America and the National Socialist White People's Party, these neo-Nazis have run candidates for office and worked to convert others to their cause. Some have cooperated with various Klan organizations, since they both hate the same enemies, believe passionately in white supremacy, and recruit from among the same pool of leaders and followers.

For propaganda purposes, some neo-Nazi organizations avoid identifying themselves as "Nazi." The best-known, best-financed, and most influential of these organizations, the Liberty Lobby, has cultivated ties to many hate groups and their leaders and promoted racist conspiracy theories. In the 1970s and 1980s the Liberty Lobby founded and nurtured the Institute for Historical Review (which produces literature denying that the Holocaust ever happened) and the Populist Party (which launched David Duke's 1988 presidential campaign). In the 1990s the Liberty Lobby has enthusiastically encouraged the militia movement. It also has published one of the nation's most widely known extreme-right publications (a weekly tabloid, called *The Spotlight*) and broadcast programming over its own radio network.

Perhaps the most influential, openly neo-Nazi organization has been National Alliance, founded in 1974 by a former publicist for the American Nazi Party, William L. Pierce. The stated goal of National Alliance has been to create all-white national enclaves, organized

Members of a neo-Nazi group riding through St. Louis, Missouri, in 1978. In the 1970s, a new generation of white supremacists embraced the ideologies, symbolism, and behavior of Adolf Hitler and his followers, which had flourished in Germany during World War II.

according to its interpretation of National Socialist principles:

> We must . . . have a racially clean area of the earth for the further development of our people. We must have White schools, White residential neighborhoods and recreation areas, White workplaces, White farms and countryside. We must have no non-Whites in our living space, and we must have open space around us for expansion.
>
> We will do whatever is necessary to achieve this White living space and to keep it White.[5]

According to National Alliance, the U.S. government has become "the single most dangerous and destructive enemy our race has ever known." It has asserted that this enemy must be replaced by "a strong, centralized government spanning several continents to coordinate many important tasks during the first few decades of a White world: the racial cleansing of the land, the rooting out of racially destructive institutions, and the reorganization of society on a new basis."[6]

One scenario for how this replacement might be accomplished was blueprinted by William Pierce in *The Turner Diaries,* a novel widely circulated among racist extremists. The book describes white revolution in late twentieth-century America and the blowing up of a federal law-enforcement building with a fertilizer-based bomb much like the one used at Oklahoma City.

Associates of Timothy McVeigh have said that *The Turner Diaries* was his favorite novel. Law-enforcement sources have told news reporters that McVeigh placed a lengthy phone call to William Pierce's private, unlisted number during the weeks just before the Oklahoma City bombing.[7]

ARYAN NATIONS, LOUIS BEAM, AND THE ORDER

Founded and led by Christian Identity minister Richard Butler, Aryan Nations has been an umbrella organization for various white supremacist factions and a vehicle for spreading the Identity "gospel."

Louis Beam, a former Klansman who became ambassador-at-large for Aryan Nations in the early 1980s, has written some of the most militant white supremacist propaganda of the 1980s and 1990s. "I'm here to tell you that if we can't have this country, as far as I'm concerned, no one gets it," Beam told a crowd in 1983. "The guns are cocked, the bullets are in the chamber. . . . We're going to fight and live or we're going to die soon."[8] Beam is credited with much of the ideological inspiration for the course of development followed by the militia movement in the 1990s.

In 1983 the Order, an offshoot of Aryan Nations, brought together several dozen Klansmen, survivalists, and neo-Nazis who shared a passionate belief in Christian Identity. They also shared the conviction that fomenting a race war/revolution was the work of God. Inspired by *The Turner Diaries,* Order members ran a successful counterfeiting operation and committed a series of murders and robberies in 1983 and 1984, including the execution of the liberal, Jewish, Denver-based radio talk-show host Alan Berg in June 1984.

By the end of the decade, law-enforcement officials had successfully shut down the Order. Fugitive Order

Excerpt from *The Militia News*

This short excerpt from an article in *The Militia News* offers a look at the kind of conspiracy theory favored by antigovernment extremists in the early 1990s. This leaflet is relatively mainstream and less explicitly racist than much militia-related literature. The article is entitled "U.S. Government Initiates Open Warfare Against American People."

There is no longer any doubt: THE U.S. GOVERN-MENT HAS DECLARED OPEN WARFARE ON THE AMERICAN PEOPLE.

The American people must know that the plan for the New World Order means total regulation and control of the people by the government—a government of tyranny which will determine what resources the people may use, what property and possessions they may have, and what and how much they will eat, where and how they will live, and even who may be permitted to live. . . .

Like lemmings, the American people are marching to their destruction. And, tragically, they seem neither to know [n]or to care! . . .

However, there are millions who have not fallen for the propaganda and conditioning, and of these millions, hundreds of thousands will physically resist even to the point of civil war, revolution, counterinsurgency, and the giving of their lives for their freedoms and their families. These are our hope. Properly informed and organized, these patriots can assure the nation's survival. . . .

—Attributed to John Grady, M.D., from *Militia News,* an undated leaflet, probably 1994 leader Robert Mathews (formerly a National Alliance recruiter) was killed when his stockpile of ammunition was ignited by flares thrown during a confrontation with police; other Order members have been sentenced to long prison terms. A wide range of white supremacists have come to view Mathews as a martyr and the imprisoned Order members as "prisoners of war" or "prisoners of the ZOG" (Zionist Occupational Government). Many have also come to view the federal government as their chief enemy—a defining characteristic of the militia movement of the 1990s.

POSSE COMITATUS

In the 1980s antigovernment extremists targeted for recruitment the many small U.S. farmers who were struggling with heavy debts, low incomes, and the threatened loss of their farms. Most farmers rejected the message of these hate groups, but some were persuaded that American family farming—and indeed all of American society—was being destroyed by an anti-white/Communist/Jewish/federal government conspiracy. Out of this combination of conspiracy theory and hard times arose the Posse Comitatus movement.

Although the movement was most active in the 1980s, the extremist ideas that took hold among those farmers attract believers even today. Posse Comitatus activists believe that the national government has no legitimate authority, and they recognize no government above the level of county sheriff. (The Latin words "posse comitatus" mean "power of the county.") For this reason, many Posse activists have refused to pay taxes—or even to register their cars—and have responded with violence to Internal Revenue Service (IRS) agents and other federal officials. Some Posse-inspired activists have committed fraud by using bogus checks and other financial documents backed by their own self-proclaimed government, a tactic the Montana Freemen took up in the 1990s. In addition to contempt for the federal government, the Posse Comitatus movement has been associated with Christian Identity beliefs, survivalism, and paramilitary training.

The best-known Posse Comitatus devotee, North Dakota farmer Gordon Kahl, refused to pay taxes, went on the lam, and killed three law-enforcement officers before he himself was killed in a shootout at his Arkansas hideout in 1983. White supremacists and tax protesters across the nation consider Kahl a martyr and a hero.

SKINHEADS

Although not all skinheads are racist, those who are have committed brutal acts of violence against blacks, Jews, Asians, Indians, Hispanics, gays, and antiracist whites across the United States. Most active and visible in the late 1980s, racist skinheads first modeled themselves on working-class British youths who shaved their heads, wore steel-toed lace-up boots, and favored aggressively racist rock music. Some American skinheads have served as security guards for neo-Nazi and other white supremacist organizations. (White Aryan Resistance, or WAR, founded by former Klansman Tom Metzger, was an especially successful magnet for racist skinheads in the 1980s. WAR reputedly received funding from the Order.) Skinheads have been encouraged in their racism and violence and targeted for recruitment by the mostly older members of various hate groups.

Chuck McCann (left), age sixteen, a skinhead recruiter in Gilroy, California, with "Bulldog" in 1989. "We haven't even done anything yet," said Chuck, "and the public is already afraid. Wait 'till we start doing something. We are the footsoldiers, the front-line warriors. We are racist, we are white nationalist, we are separatist, and we work with the Klan and with the American Nazi Party. We live, we eat, sleep, breathe and talk skinhead.... Our goal now is to recruit—to get all the people who haven't already linked on."

All of these organizations, individuals, and beliefs have provided inspiration, leadership, and/or recruits for the militia movement of the 1990s. But the modern militia movement has drawn on a much wider segment of American society than the extremist fringe of isolated hate groups. The militias have successfully reached into the American mainstream to find recruits and supporters.

CHAPTER TWO

From Mainstream America to the Militia Extreme

"It's like a funnel moving through space. At the front end, it's picking up lots and lots of people by hitting on issues that have wide appeal, like gun control and environmental restrictions, which enrage many people here out West. Then you go a little bit further into the funnel, and it's about ideology, about the oppressiveness of the federal government. Then, further in, . . . it's about the anti-Semitic conspiracy. Finally, at the narrowest end of the funnel, you've drawn in the hard core, where you get someone like Tim McVeigh popping out. . . . The bigger the front end of the funnel is, the bigger the number that get to the core."

Ken Toole,
Montana Human Rights Network [1]

In recent years, several events and conditions have increased the reach and pull of the "funnel" from mainstream America to the militia extreme. The most obvious phenomenon has been the increased media visibility of individuals and of hate groups that are expressing more-mainstream antiliberal points of view. From David Duke in the 1970s, to neo-Nazi skinheads in the 1980s, to anti-government militants in the 1990s, diverse hatemongers have succeeded in gaining national exposure for themselves on television in return for providing colorful, sensational material that boosts the ratings of talk shows and other programs.

In the 1980s and 1990s the popularity of talk radio rose greatly, dominated by such antiliberal national on-air personalities as Rush Limbaugh, Pat Buchanan, and G. Gordon Liddy. Liddy is a former Federal Bureau of Investigation (FBI) agent and White House official who went to jail in the early 1970s for his role in the Watergate affair, which forced President Richard Nixon to resign from office. While Limbaugh has had the largest audience, Liddy has captured the imagination of militia supporters:

> You have every right to fear your government. Look at what the brutal thugs of the Bureau of Alcohol, Tobacco and Firearms do, smashing into homes, shooting as they come in, killing people. When they don't do that, they *trash* the home, *steal* the money from the people who have *never* been accused of a crime, take their possessions, *stomp* the cat to death on the way out, then threaten the wife that if she talks about it, *that they'll be back,* that they're federal agents—they can do *anything they want to do.* . . . You'd better be afraid of 'em! [2]

Don't aim a gun at an ATF agent's chest, Liddy once suggested on the air, "because they got a [bulletproof]

The extreme antigovernment views of G. Gordon Liddy, convicted mastermind of the Watergate scandal during Richard Nixon's administration, appeal to militia supporters.

vest on underneath that. Head shots. Head shots. . . . Kill the sons of bitches!"[3]

Even more extreme points of view have been found on local-access cable television and on local and short-wave radio programs. The Liberty Lobby has produced several programs, as have other hate groups. Some have sounded surprisingly reasonable on the air, according to one journalist who monitors right-wing extremism. On shortwave radio, for example, "you could get a marvelous program from the National Alliance which sounds very reasonable until you send away for their literature, which is neo-Nazi. It sounds populist on the air, but it comes with swastikas in a plain brown wrapper."[4]

Other programs have sounded less reasonable. Timothy McVeigh was a fan of the militia-oriented radio personality Mark Koernke (also known as "Mark from Michigan"). In the early 1990s, Koernke broadcast a nightly "Intelligence Report" on shortwave, spinning elaborate conspiracy theories, urging his listeners to arm themselves to fight against encroaching government tyranny, and signing off with: "God bless the republic, death to the new world order, we shall prevail."[5] In addition to his radio program, Koernke has also marketed audio recordings and videotapes of his speeches, which have been sold along with a host of other militia-oriented motivational materials through mail order and at gun shows and militia gatherings.

Many hate groups have learned to use electronic technology for propaganda purposes. Some have answering machines with recorded hate messages. Computers have opened up a whole new world of hate-group communications by enabling activists to desktop-publish their own

Mark Koernke, also known as "Mark from Michigan," is a leading advocate of the militia movement and urges militia members to prepare for war.

literature. Many organizations and individuals have also maintained computer bulletin boards for relatively private and secure yet extensively networked communications. Some have dramatically expanded the reach of their influence by creating their own World Wide Web sites and Internet mailing lists, and by participating in on-line newsgroups.

ECONOMIC AND SOCIAL CHANGES

In recent years, many Americans have become anxious about their economic futures. Are their jobs secure, or will they be "downsized" out of work, through no fault of their own? If they lose their jobs, will they ever find other ones that pay as well? Will they ever be able to afford to retire? Do their children face an even bleaker economic future? Coupled with these economic anxieties has been widespread uncertainty about the wisdom of social changes that have taken place over the past several decades—changes in the roles and opportunities for women, enforcement of civil rights for blacks and other minorities, greater acceptance of homosexuals, extensive protection of the environment, and the loss of privacy due to increasingly interlinked recordkeeping by government and corporations.

Hate groups have aggressively recruited white men who share these anxieties and doubts. The reason behind all of their problems, the recruiters say, is that white American men have been the victims of a conspiracy against them. The details of the conspiracy, and of the solutions they propose, vary somewhat from group to group, but the common thread is hate: hatred of blacks, of homosexuals, of independent women, of

Jews, of "foreigners," of the mainstream media, and of the federal government, which is depicted as an oppressive tyrant.

Hatemongers often gain access by offering solidarity and mutual support for people who feel that they're going through unfairly hard times. Most people reject the extremists' explanations and invitations to blame their problems on scapegoats. But many think that there might be some truth in what they say. Some are willing to move a little farther into the funnel to learn more. The theories may begin to feel more comfortable and seem less far-fetched as these newcomers make friends and find a social life among conspiracy theorists.

ENVIRONMENTAL POLICY CHANGES

In the 1970s, as the environmental movement took hold, the federal government passed clean air laws, clean water laws, and many other environmental regulations. While most environmental legislation enjoyed wide and enthusiastic public support, many business owners felt that at least some of these regulations were too great and intrusive a burden. The early 1980s brought a "Sagebrush Rebellion" to national prominence—a loosely organized coalition of Western ranchers and miners who had been accustomed (some for generations) to using federal lands more or less as they saw fit and who resented federal efforts to manage those lands to protect the environment. One of their own activists, James Watt, aggressively pursued their interests (and infuriated environmentalists) as secretary of the Interior Department under President Ronald Reagan. During the three Reagan-Bush administrations, access to many federal lands and resources was cheap and virtually unrestricted.

When Bill Clinton took office at the beginning of 1993, however, environmental protection became a higher priority, and resentment of environmental and other governmental regulation grew. This time, the coalition opposing Washington has taken several approaches. Some groups have lobbied for "wise use" or "multiple use" of public lands—a balance of economic, environmental, and recreational uses. (Many of these advocates have been funded by businesses with large commercial interests in resources located on public lands.) Others have pushed to expand private property rights to require the government to pay property owners compensation whenever any government regulation, such as restrictions on the use of wetlands, affects the value of an owner's property. A few have actually gained control of county governments and attempted to seize federal lands and place them under complete control of local residents.

What all of these activists and their supporters have had in common is that they have encouraged, especially in the West, resentment of and hostility toward the federal government and federal agents. "The second violent American revolution is just about—I got my fingers about a quarter of an inch apart—is just about that far away," said Rush Limbaugh in February 1995. "Because these people are sick and tired of a bunch of bureaucrats in Washington driving into town and telling them what they can and can't do with their land." [6] Strident rhetoric such as this, from a successful, nationally syndicated radio host, has made it more acceptable to see the federal government as "the enemy." It has widened the mouth of the funnel.

More-extreme activists for property rights and local control have mingled with militia members and other extremists who see the federal government as an occupying army. Some property rights/local control activists, mostly in remote parts of the West, have set up enclaves where they refuse to recognize any federal government authority at all. Others have intimidated federal workers—judges, agents of the Bureau of Land Management, even forest rangers—and threatened them with violence. Forest Service outposts have been bombed. Routine maintenance work has been halted in some areas for fear of violence.

One property-rights publication headlined its October 1994 issue this way: "Why There Is a Need for the Militia in America." It went on to state: "We realize that our urban cousins appear to be basically ignorant as to what is going on in the property rights sector. But one need only to have the IQ of tree bark to realize the federal government is out of control. Could this be a time for the militia?"[7]

THE INFLUENCE OF
THE CHRISTIAN RIGHT

The politically active, socially conservative "Christian right" has also connected mainstream America to extremists deep in the funnel. The most obvious connection has been through the militant wing of the antiabortion movement. Antiabortion militants have bombed and vandalized abortion clinics across the nation, murdered doctors and clinic staff members, and waged a decades-long campaign of civil disobedience, courting arrest for blocking clinic entrances and for similar direct actions. Like militia activists, antiabortion militants have seen themselves as being actually at war with a government that sanctions and supports fundamentally immoral values.

Popular antiliberal radio personality Rush Limbaugh uses his program to express resentment of the federal government. He predicts that "the second violent American Revolution" is not far away.

Some antiabortion militants have networked with militia supporters directly. Larry Pratt, a militia-friendly antigun-control activist, has solicited money through his Committee to Protect the Family to help fund the antiabortion organization Operation Rescue, which has specialized in demonstrations intended to shut down abortion clinics. Randall Terry, the founder of Operation Rescue, was photographed onstage at a rally with militia activists. Antiabortion activist Mathew Trewhella told a militia rally in 1994 that parents should arm their children with "an SKS rifle and 500 rounds of ammunition." [8]

Many white supremacists have woven opposition to abortion into their racist agenda, as in this recorded message:

> Almost all abortion doctors are Jews. Abortion makes money for Jews. Almost all abortion nurses are lesbians. Abortion gives thrills to lesbians. Abortion. . . is promoted by the corrupt Jewish organization called Planned Parenthood. The name, alone, proves their corruption because they don't plan parents, they plot the murder of innocent white children. . . . Jews must be punished for this holocaust and murder of white children along with their perverted lesbian nurses who enjoy their jobs too much.
>
> You have reached WAR. . .White Aryan Resistance. [9]

The Christian right has created or enabled other links to the funnel as well. Through intemperate rhetoric and aggressive efforts to make the Christian right's version of morality the law of the land, prominent conservative preachers have effectively encouraged their listeners to view the principle of live-and-let-live as immoral. In this way, the mainstream Christian right has made respectable a notion common among extremists deep within the funnel—that many of America's social norms and legal protections are morally wrong.

The Christian right also has shared with extremists a receptiveness to conspiracy theory and a tendency to assign sinister qualities to Jews. Both are on prominent display in *The New World Order*, the bestselling book by Pat Robertson, television evangelist and founder of the Christian Coalition, the nation's largest and most powerful Christian-right organization.

In this book, Robertson echoes the conspiracy theorists of the far-right fringe. Although Robertson staunchly supports Israel, he peppers his writing with anti-Semitic rhetoric and assigns Jews disproportionate blame for the world's ills. The central idea of his book is that an international Freemason-Communist-banker conspiracy, dominated by Jews, has shaped the course of world history in this century for sinister ends. This conspiracy, according to Robertson's interpretation of the biblical book of Revelation, is propelling the world toward Armageddon:

> A single thread runs from the White House to the State Department to the Council on Foreign Relations to the Trilateral Commission to secret societies to extreme New Agers. There must be a new world order. It must eliminate national sovereignty. There must be world government,

a world police force, world courts, world banking and currency, and a world elite in charge of it all. . . .

Can it be that the phrase the *new world order* means something entirely different to the inner circle of a secret society than it does to the ordinary person?. . . Indeed, it may well be that men of goodwill. . . are in reality unknowingly and unwittingly carrying out the mission and mouthing the phrases of a tightly knit cabal whose goal is nothing less than a new order for the human race under the domination of Lucifer and his followers. . . .

For the past two hundred years the term *new world order* has been the code phrase of those who desired to destroy the Christian faith and . . . replace it with an occult-inspired world socialist dictatorship. . . .

Rest assured, there is a behind-the-scenes Establishment in this nation, as in every other. It has enormous power. It has controlled the economic and foreign policy objectives of the United States for the past seventy years. . . . Beyond the control of wealth, its principal goal is the establishment of a one-world government where the control of money is in the hands of one or more privately owned but government-chartered central banks. . . .

For years, to further their utopian one-world plans, they have been trying to undermine American education, moral values, sense of patriotism and national pride. . . .

It is as if a giant plan is unfolding, everything perfectly on cue . . . .

The new world order will have as its religion a god of light, whom Bible scholars recognize as Lucifer." [10]

Robertson's worldview, the language that he uses (including "new world order"), and the details of the conspiracy he outlines overlap with the conspiracy theories found deep in the funnel. A popular and influential figure, he has lent the extremists a share of his own mainstream respectability, and some plausibility as well.

CHANGES ON THE POLITICAL SCENE

In the mid-1970s, antiabortion activism began to grow in response to *Roe* v. *Wade* (the 1973 Supreme Court decision legalizing abortion). At the same time, right-wing Republican party activists stepped up their efforts to reach out to socially conservative voters concerned about what they perceived as a decline in American family life and morality. As they drew large numbers of the growing Christian right into politics—and into a lasting alliance with the Republican party—these right-wing activists nudged aside the more moderate Republicans who had long dominated the party's leadership. The 1980 national elections brought Ronald Reagan to the White House, a Republican majority to the Senate, and the Christian right to the foreground of national politics.

Throughout the 1980s and into the 1990s, the Christian right became more practiced at delivering votes for conservative candidates, and its influence over the Republican party grew. Hard-line opposition to abortion and support for a socially conservative agenda increasingly became the Republican party line.

By the 1992 presidential election campaign, the Republican party had been transformed. The Republican national convention that year was dominated by such extreme cultural conservatives as Pat Buchanan. In his prime-time convention speech, Buchanan took swipes at homosexuals, "radical feminism," and assorted liberal Democrats. Then, echoing Nazi German rhetoric, Buchanan asserted: "There is a religious war going on in our country for the soul of America. It is a cultural war." The chief image that Buchanan chose to illustrate this war was that of U.S. troops versus black rioters in Los Angeles: "And as they took back the streets of L.A., block by block, so must we take back our cities, and take back our culture, and take back our country. God bless you, and God bless America." [11] To white supremacists, this sounded like race war.

Militia supporters share many of Buchanan's values. They think that we are in a cultural war, too—a real, shooting war.

CHAPTER THREE

Ruby Ridge, Waco, and the Issue of Gun Control

"A well-regulated Militia, being necessary to the security of a free State, the right of the People to keep and bear Arms, shall not be infringed.**"**

> Second Amendment to
> the U.S. Constitution

The ideology of hate groups together with various changes in mainstream American politics and culture provided the fuel for the militia movement of the 1990s. The sparks that set it off were two key events—the 1992 shootout at Randy Weaver's home at Ruby Ridge, Idaho, and the 1993 conflagration at the Branch Davidian compound near Waco, Texas—and one contentious issue, gun control.

RUBY RIDGE

Randy Weaver, a survivalist living on Ruby Ridge, a remote mountain in Idaho, was indicted by a federal grand jury in December 1990 for selling two illegally sawed-off shotguns to a government informer in 1989. Weaver has claimed that the government entrapped him.

The government had targeted Weaver for investigation because of his ties to the well-armed white supremacist/Christian Identity organization Aryan Nations. Aryan Nations is based in northern Idaho, where its members have long sought to establish an all-white "homeland." Although Weaver was not formally a member of the group, he had several times visited the Aryan Nations compound, about 60 miles (97 kilometers) from Weaver's home, and an informer had told the government that Weaver wanted to sell guns to the group.

After his indictment, Weaver holed up with his wife, Vicki, and their children at their mountaintop home. Kevin Harris, a family friend in his early twenties who had been informally adopted by Randy Weaver some years earlier, also lived with them there. "Whether we live or whether we die," the Weavers wrote in a letter, "we will not obey your lawless government." [1]

For some years, the Weavers had been largely self-sufficient, in preparation for the impending Armageddon predicted by Christian Identity preachers. After Randy's arraignment, they didn't leave their mountaintop at all. Friends kept them supplied with food and delivered their mail. To avoid risking a violent confrontation with the well-armed Weaver (and perhaps his three school-age children, who had been seen carrying weapons near their home), federal marshals decided to watch and wait. They waited for more than a year and a half.

Then, on Friday, August 21, 1992, shots rang out as federal agents were making one of their regular visits to the heavily wooded mountaintop to check on the Weaver home. One deputy marshal was killed.

Federal officials from the U.S. Marshal Service, the Federal Bureau of Investigation (FBI), and the Bureau

White separatist Randy Weaver, being sworn in before a Senate subcommittee after the Ruby Ridge incident.

Randy Weaver surrendered to federal authorities after the eleven-day standoff at the Weaver home on Ruby Ridge, in Idaho. The confiscated guns and ammunition were displayed outside the home as media members and federal agents roamed the site.

of Alcohol, Tobacco and Firearms sent helicopters, armored vehicles, and hostage-rescue experts to the scene. Altogether, a small army of nearly 200 police officers and federal agents was deployed.

Some of the Weavers' neighbors, many of whom had supported the Weavers during the long siege, gathered to protest against the agents at roadblocks set up near the Weavers' cabin. Many were self-identified white supremacists, including a few skinheads sporting swastikas. Others were simply neighbors who believed that the federal government had overstepped its rightful authority. "Randy Weaver just wanted to be left alone, but the Government went after his property, after his firearms, and now they're paying for it," one protester said. "That man, Randy Weaver, is a patriot, not a criminal." [2]

On Saturday, August 22, following unusually permissive rules for using deadly force, an FBI sharpshooter fired two shots as Randy Weaver, his daughter Sara, and Kevin Harris ran from federal agents into the cabin. It was not clear to the FBI at the time whether anyone had been hit, and information about this second round of gunfire was not immediately released to the press.

On Sunday, two days after the initial gunfight, federal agents found the body of fourteen-year-old Samuel Weaver in a shed near the cabin. He apparently had been killed in the first exchange of gunshots, which had also killed the deputy marshal.

The standoff at Ruby Ridge drew national attention. It also drew Bo Gritz, a former Green Beret who had become a prominent figure among antigovernment activists, survivalists, and Identity believers, as well as an adviser for the Liberty Lobby. (Timothy McVeigh passed some of Gritz's literature on to an old army buddy.) At the time of the Ruby Ridge standoff, Gritz was running for president on the ticket of the Populist Party, which had previously nominated the neo-Nazi former KKK leader David Duke for president. ("Gritz. Rhymes with whites," his campaign workers said. [3])

Gritz and his colleague Jack McLamb volunteered to mediate between Weaver and federal agents. (McLamb, a former police officer, has aggressively recruited for the militia movement among active-duty police officers.) On Friday, a week after the initial shooting that had killed his son, Randy Weaver allowed Gritz to approach the cabin for a talk. Gritz learned that when the FBI sniper had fired at them on the previous Saturday, Randy Weaver had been lightly wounded, Kevin Harris had been gravely wounded, and Vicki Weaver had been instantly killed, while standing just inside the door of the cabin and holding her ten-month-old baby girl in her arms. Vicki's body remained in the cabin with her husband, Kevin Harris, the baby, and the Weavers' twelve- and sixteen-year-old daughters.

Sunday, ten days into the standoff, Kevin Harris surrendered. He was coughing up blood, his gunshot wounds were infected, and he needed immediate medical attention. He later would face trial for murdering the deputy marshal who died in the initial shootout.

The next day, Randy Weaver himself surrendered. "He just cried his wife's name, his son's name, and he stood up tall like a man, and we marched tall down the road like we said we were going to," said Bo Gritz, who walked out of the cabin with Weaver after helping to negotiate his surrender. [4] Weaver was taken into custody and eventually charged with firearms violations, failure to appear for trial, and aiding and abetting the murder of the deputy marshal.

Nearly a year later, in 1993, both Weaver and Harris were acquitted in the death of the deputy marshal. Weaver was also acquitted of the original firearms charges against him, but convicted of failing to appear to stand trial in 1991.

By this time, Randy Weaver and the events at Ruby Ridge had become a rallying point for antigovernment militia recruiters. Many Americans felt that the Weaver family had been the victims of an arrogant federal government using excessive force and overstepping its legitimate bounds. Militia propagandists effectively fit Ruby Ridge into a broader and deadly pattern of federal government tyranny, a pattern made more dangerous by new gun-control measures and crowned by awful events near Waco, Texas, in 1993.

WACO

The Branch Davidian sect was a small offshoot of the Seventh Day Adventists led by self-styled messiah David Koresh (also known as Vernon Howell). Dozens of Branch Davidians, including many children, lived with Koresh in the sect's isolated compound located just outside of Waco, Texas. There they hoarded food and other supplies, armed themselves heavily, and prepared for Armageddon.

On February 28, 1993, after months of investigation, federal agents from the Bureau of Alcohol, Tobacco and Firearms raided the Branch Davidian compound, seeking to arrest David Koresh on weapons charges. The ATF agents were met with gunfire, which they returned. Four agents were killed. Six Branch Davidians died also, although this was not known for certain until much later. David Koresh apparently was wounded, though not seriously. The ATF was sharply criticized for carrying out the raid even though it seemed that Koresh had learned that they were coming.

After the failed raid, hundreds of federal agents surrounded the compound, and a long siege began. The agents shone bright lights and blasted bizarre musical and other recordings at the Branch Davidians. As at Ruby Ridge the year before, the siege drew national news coverage as well as the attention of militia-oriented antigovernment activists. Louis Beam traveled to Waco during the siege. So did Timothy McVeigh.

Negotiations with Koresh took place off and on, but seemed to go nowhere. Thirty-seven people, including 21 children and 2 men who had sneaked into the compound after the siege began, eventually left the compound. David Koresh said that 95 people remained inside.

On April 19, 1993, 51 days after the siege had begun, federal agents in armored vehicles approached the compound and began to pump tear gas into it, in an effort to drive everyone out of the building. Almost immediately, fires started in several places. As the building burned to the ground, punctuated by a big blast (believed to be the sect's ammunition exploding), only 9 people escaped from the building. Approximately 80 others, including perhaps as many as 20 children, died in the blaze.

The fire that consumed the compound was set by the Branch Davidians themselves, investigators later concluded, based on videotapes of the event and evidence found at the scene. (Several of those who escaped during

The Branch Davidian compound in Waco, Texas, where followers of David Koresh had been surrounded by federal agents for 51 days, goes up in flames. Of the estimated nearly 100 people inside the compound, there were only 9 survivors.

the fire confirmed this; others denied it.) David Koresh's body was found in the ruins, with one bullet wound in the middle of his forehead. Some of the other bodies were also marked with bullet holes.

Even though most Americans believed that David Koresh was a madman and that the Branch Davidians had committed mass suicide, many also believed that the government had botched the whole affair, and that if it had been handled differently, so many people might not have died. Attorney General Janet Reno, who had approved the decision to pump tear gas into the compound, took full responsibility for the action. Speaking on television the night of April 19, she said the assault on the compound that morning had been "based on what we knew then. Based on what we know now, it was obviously wrong. Obviously, if I thought the chances were great of a mass suicide, I would never have approved the plan." [5]

Most Americans watching the events at Waco considered the Branch Davidians to be deranged and dangerous cult members confronting a basically well-meaning federal government that made terrible mistakes with tragic consequences. Many Americans, however, primed by anti-government conspiracy theories, saw the tragedy—occurring only months after the Randy Weaver standoff—as further evidence that the federal government had become dangerously tyrannical.

Kirk Lyons, a white supremacist attorney who offered assistance to both Randy Weaver and the Branch Davidians, declared:

Every American should be interested in what happened at Waco. The issue is: are we going to allow the government to surround us in our homes and churches and burn us to the ground—and kill us? That's the issue! It's nothing more complicated than that! Are we going to allow the government, using spurious charges, to polish off people that don't agree with its policies, and allow it to lie through it's [*sic*] teeth for fifty-one days; and then, allow it to get away with murder? . . .

We see the Waco case as nothing more or less than evidence of an ongoing pattern of federal abuse and murder. It's been going on for many years, but has not been noticed by the average citizen, because the number of casualties has generally been so minimal.

I mean, when you polish off . . . any of these so-called "white separatist kooks"—which is the way they've been portrayed by the media—most Americans say "good riddance." Unfortunately, the average American does not recognize these incidents as evidence of a pattern of ongoing federal abuse.

Consider the Weaver case. They killed a nursing mother holding a ten-month-old baby in her arms, and blew away a fourteen-year-old boy. Well, everyone's consciousness was heightened as a result of that. Now, we go one step further. We incinerate almost one hundred innocent men, women, and children—in their church! And the government, at least in the short term, has gotten away with it. Most people have bought the government line. . . .

But as time goes on, the truth will come out. And whatever the final historical opinion of Koresh is, I think it will ultimately be shown that the government was by far the greater criminal in this case. And that whatever punishment David Koresh may have deserved, he certainly didn't deserve what he got, nor did the innocent women and children who were incinerated and who died a horrible and painful death at the hands of a callous and insensitive government. [6]

Woven into this kind of reasoning, the Waco tragedy became one of the most effective recruiting tools used by antigovernment militias and related hate groups.

GUN CONTROL

Waco was put to similar use by the National Rifle Association (NRA) in its ongoing campaign to block any kind of gun-control legislation. Although the NRA is considered a mainstream organization (and one of the most effective lobbying organizations in the halls of Congress), it has often used the kind of rhetoric favored by militia organizers and other extremists. Just after Waco, for example, a member of the NRA's board of directors wrote:

How long are the American people going to put up with this sort of thing? It is popular at this time to compare the behavior of our uncontrolled Federal agents to that of the Nazis in the Third Reich. . . . But the Nazis are long ago and far away, whereas the ninja in the U.S. are right now in full cry and apparently without fear of any sort of control. They move mainly at night. They conceal their faces. They use overwhelming firepower and they make almost no effort to identify their targets. They are scarier than the Nazis.[7]

The most important single issue for antigovernment militias has been their completely unrestricted interpretation of the right to "keep and bear arms" specified in the Second Amendment to the U.S. Constitution, an interpretation they share with the NRA. This issue has drawn most of the mainstream recruits into the militias, and far-fringe hate activists have effectively exploited the highly charged issue of gun control to draw susceptible individuals deeper into the funnel. Neo-Nazi leader William Pierce wrote in February 1994:

> The current campaign . . . to disarm Americans has many people angrier than anyone might imagine who is not in touch with what might be called "the weapons culture." What this means is we have a great opportunity now to make an impression on a very receptive audience, if we move aggressively and use a reasonable degree of discretion.
> Gun shows provide a natural recruiting environment. Many more are being held now than ever before, and many more people are attending them.[8]

In the early 1990s, the federal government passed two key pieces of gun-control legislation that the militias and other extremists have depicted as part of a wider campaign intended to disarm the American people so that they will be unable to defend themselves against growing government tyranny: the Brady bill and the assault weapons ban.

Signed into law in November 1993, the Brady bill requires that people wait five days before buying a handgun, during which time local police are to check the background of the prospective buyer to screen out anyone not permitted to buy handguns (including convicted felons, minors, substance abusers, and illegal immigrants).

The assault weapons ban was signed into law in September 1994 as part of an omnibus anticrime bill. This measure imposed a ten-year ban on the manufacture, sale, and possession of certain specified semiautomatic guns (others were explicitly exempted from the ban) as well as certain forms of ammunition that allow more than ten shots before reloading. Gun owners were permitted to keep assault weapons that they already owned legally.

Not only the militias but also the "mainstream" NRA depicted these measures as part of a comprehensive effort to take away *all* of the constitutional rights and liberties of patriotic Americans. Both used lurid language to demonize government workers:

> The semi-auto ban gives jackbooted Government thugs more power to take away our Constitutional rights, break in our doors, seize our guns, destroy our property and even injure or kill us. . . .
>
> In Clinton's Administration, if you have a badge, you have the Government's go-ahead to harass, intimidate, or even murder law-abiding citizens. . . .

The interpretation of the Constitutional right to "keep and bear arms" has been a central issue for anitgovernment militias, which oppose gun-control legislation, such as the Brady bill, signed by President Bill Clinton on November 30, 1993. The bill is named for Bill Brady, shown here seated next to the President. Brady, who was President Ronald Reagan's press secretary, was seriously injured in an assassination attempt made on President Reagan on March 30, 1981.

You can see it when jackbooted Government thugs, wearing black, armed to the teeth, break down a door, open fire with an automatic weapon and kill or maim law-abiding citizens. . . .

And if we lose the right to keep and bear arms, then the right to free speech, free practice of religion and every other freedom in the Bill of Rights are soon to follow. [9]

The executive vice president of the NRA wrote these lines in a fundraising letter dated April 13, 1995. Less than a week later, scores of these so-called government thugs died in the bombing at Oklahoma City—two years to the day after the fire at Waco.

CHAPTER FOUR

The Militia Movement of the 1990s

"The common thread that unites the . . . groups we watch, and which brings a little cohesiveness to an otherwise disconnected movement, is an extreme hatred for the Federal Government. . . . I think they're heartened by how much mainstream citizens seem to be voicing the same thing. They feel this is their time. It's their time to make hay.**"**

> Danny Welch, director of the
> Southern Poverty Law Center's
> Klanwatch project [1]

The events at Ruby Ridge and Waco, together with the gun-control legislation of the early 1990s, nudged many Americans into believing that their government poses a danger to them, their families, and their communities. From the time of the Ruby Ridge standoff in 1992 to the Oklahoma City bombing in 1995, tens of thousands joined antigovernment militia organizations that sprang up across the country. Some of these militias were small cells with only a few members; others boasted a thousand or more members; many cultivated links to white supremacist hate groups. In addition to the core of actual militia members, many more people sympathized with and supported the values and goals of the militias.

LEADERLESS RESISTANCE
As the militia movement began to grow, hate activists fueled its growth through propaganda, networking, and other means, and targeted its members for recruitment into more extreme forms of activism. Leaders of some of America's most vicious hate groups adopted a strategy for pulling susceptible, but not yet fanatical, militia members and supporters deeper into the funnel: leaderless resistance, a movement of committed individuals and small groups who share the same propaganda, information, and goals, but have no formal chain of command.

In October 1992, less than two months after Randy Weaver surrendered at Ruby Ridge, dozens of extremists from Aryan Nations and other Identity organizations, various Klan groups, and other hate groups, met in Estes Park, Colorado, at the invitation of the prominent Christian Identity preacher Pete Peters. They planned to talk about the Weaver incident and to discuss coordinating their strategies. Those attending ranged from the relatively mainstream Larry Pratt, founder of Gun Owners of America and a well-connected and effective Washington lobbyist, to revolutionary white supremacist Louis Beam. Many Christian Identity believers were there, but so were Baptists, Presbyterians, and Mennonites.

Many of these groups and individuals had serious disagreements and had shunned one another in the past; Ruby Ridge, however, had brought them together. Unity—and mainstream acceptability—was also fostered at the meeting by the restraint on racist rhetoric showed there even by well-known white supremacists. Instead of ranting about "satanic Jews" and "niggers," everyone at the meeting focused on one enemy: the federal government. "I warn you calmly, coldly, and without reservation that over the next ten years you will come to hate government more than anything in your life," Beam, the keynote speaker, told the conference. [2]

A consensus emerged at Estes Park that militias organized by citizens and completely independent of state and federal government were necessary and should establish themselves across the country as a defense against federal tyranny. (The militia movement was just beginning at this point. It really took off after Waco.) Networking connections made between activists during the three-day meeting enabled them to work on organizing these militias more efficiently and effectively than anyone would have thought possible only a few months before.

Many of the activists at Estes Park also endorsed— then went home and put into action—the general organizing strategy of leaderless resistance. This strategy had been enthusiastically promoted by Louis Beam in an article he had published early in 1992, which became one of the most popular pieces of literature on the militia circuit. Beam wrote that leaderless resistance, or "phantom cell" organization,

> does not have any central control or direction. . . . All individuals and groups operate independently of each other, and never report to a central headquarters or single leader for direction or instruction. . . .

Louis Beam is escorted away from a news briefing after the Waco incident in 1993, having been arrested for disruptive behavior.

Participants in a program of leaderless resistance through "Phantom cell" or individual action must know exactly what they are doing and how to do it. . . .

Since the entire purpose of leaderless resistance is to defeat state tyranny, . . . all members of phantom cells or individuals will tend to react to objective events in the same way through usual tactics of resistance. Organs of information distribution such as newspapers, leaflets, computers, etc., which are widely available to all, keep each person informed of events, allowing for a planned response that will take many variations. No one need issue an order to anyone. Those idealists truly committed to the cause of freedom will act when they feel the time is ripe, or will take their cue from others who precede them. . . .

It goes almost without saying that leaderless resistance leads to very small or even one-man cells of resistance. . . . For those who are serious about their opposition to federal despotism, this is exactly what is desired. . . .

The LAST thing federal snoops want, if they had any choice in the matter, is a thousand different small phantom cells opposing them. It is easy to see why. . . . Leaderless resistance presents no single opportunity for the Federals to destroy a significant portion of the resistance. . . .

The federal government is preparing the way for a major assault upon those persons opposed to their policies. . . .

Let the coming night be filled with a thousand points of resistance. Like the fog which forms when conditions are right, and disappears when they are not, so must the resistance to tyranny be. [3]

THE NEW MILITIAS

The new militias of the 1990s differed from many of the hate groups of the 1980s and earlier. The new militias were open, not secret, organizations. Anybody opposed to gun control and concerned about a threat to citizens' freedom posed by the federal government was welcome to join the new militias and participate in paramilitary training exercises.

Although the militias attracted racists and often networked with explicitly racist organizations, the glue that held militia members together was not white supremacy but rather hatred of the federal government and fear of a "New World Order" conspiracy. Keeping racism off to the side undoubtedly made the militias attractive to a much larger group of potential recruits (even a few black recruits, in some militias). So did the militia concerns that overlapped with those held by mainstream America about the direction in which the country was headed. For these and perhaps other reasons as well, even though most of the militias of the 1990s were small, local organizations, vastly more people became involved in them than had been in the explicitly racist hate groups of the 1960s, 1970s, and 1980s.

What, exactly, were these new militias up to? Many organized themselves into local, independent military chains of command and engaged in paramilitary training, such as target practice and surveillance. Most militia participants used their own guns, which were often standard hunting equipment. Some militias, however, stockpiled weapons, including military-style assault rifles, armor-piercing ammunition, hand grenades, land mines, and bulk explosives.

Militia members also cultivated ties with potential recruits and with other militia organizations, creating an informal national network of like-minded individuals intended to offer mutual assistance should the government escalate its "war" against them. Much of this networking was accomplished at gun shows and similar gatherings. Many militia activists kept in touch through computer bulletin boards and e-mail, and similar, often identical, propaganda literature circulated through militias across the country. Much of this literature featured variations on the same sorts of conspiracy theories favored by white supremacists. Great quantities of literature circulated among militias were produced by hate groups themselves.

WHO AND WHERE ARE THE MILITIA GROUPS?

The following are some of the militia groups and leaders that have been most active and influential in the 1990s.

United States Militia Association. Idaho harbors the Aryan Nations compound, visited by Randy Weaver, and Almost Heaven, the armed "Christian Covenant Community" established by Bo Gritz. It also has been home to one of the earliest of the nation's new militia organizations, Samuel Sherwood's United States Militia Association. Sherwood, who by the end of 1994 had organized militia groups in at least twelve Idaho counties and whose literature circulated well beyond his home state, favored conspiracy theories and was deeply suspicious of the federal government. President Clinton, he said, "was determined to seize your guns, steal your food, take your children away. In his term he will have killed more babies than Hitler, put more homosexuals in government than Sodom and Gomorrah, had the schools teach your children it is right and forced you to accept it." [4]

For a while in the early 1990s, Sherwood took the unusual tack of selectively supporting certain politicians, with the apparent intent of gaining favorable press coverage and legitimacy—and more recruits—for his militia and also, perhaps, of influencing legislators to pass laws favoring his agenda. Whatever gains he might have made with lawmakers were largely undone in March 1995, when he was quoted urging supporters to "go up and look legislators in the face, because someday you may be forced to blow it off." [5]

Also in March 1995, just before the Oklahoma City bombing, Sherwood voiced what militia activists all over the country were abuzz with at the time—a wave of rumors that the federal government was about to launch a crackdown against militia groups. (The rumors were especially rife on the Internet, which is an ideal medium for rumor-mongering.) "The rumors are flying," Sherwood said, "about pending attacks on 'militias' in Montana, Florida, and Michigan. The rumor mill won't stop, and sooner or later the 'Cold War' between the federal bureaucracy and the states will escalate into a shooting war." [6]

Bo Gritz, former Green Beret and founder of the armed "Christian Covenant Community," at a militia gathering.

Linda Thompson and the Unorganized Militia of the United States. Linda Thompson, a lawyer and a U.S. Army veteran based in Indianapolis, has called herself "Acting Adjunct General" of the "Unorganized Militia of the United States." A one-woman clearinghouse for militia information (via mail, fax, radio, and the Internet, as well as in person at militia gatherings), Thompson has claimed to be in touch with militias in all fifty states.

Like many militia activists, Thompson was galvanized into action by the tragedy at the Branch Davidian complex near Waco. She produced and has sold two videos popular on the militia circuit, *Waco, the Big Lie* and *Waco II—The Big Lie Continues,* which assert that federal agents used flamethrowers to start the fire at Waco. (Timothy McVeigh sent a copy of *Waco, the Big Lie* to an old army buddy.) Thompson has been a frequent speaker at gun shows and other militia-related events.

In 1994, Thompson attempted to organize a mass march on Washington by militia members from across the country, armed and in uniform, to deliver to the government a "Declaration of Independence" and to arrest any members of Congress failing to conform with an "Ultimatum" sent to them by Thompson earlier that year, on April 19, the first anniversary of the Waco conflagration. This ultimatum featured many elements of New World Order conspiracy theory and Posse Comitatus jargon. It demanded, among other things, that Congress repeal the Brady bill and the 14th, 16th, and 17th Amendments to the U.S. Constitution. The ultimatum also demanded that Congress:

Declare that the United States of America is not operating under the authority of the United Nations. . . .

Declare the federal debt to the Federal Reserve null and void. . . .

Declare that the federal government does not now have and never has had the legal authority to enact or enforce criminal laws outside the area of Washington, D.C. . . .

Convene a full Congressional inquiry . . . into the events in Waco. . . .

Notice: *You have until 8:00 a.m., September 19, 1994,* . . . to personally initiate legislation to this effect and to do all things necessary to effect this legislation and the restoration of a Constitutional government within this country.

If you do not personally and publicly attend to these demands, you will be identified as a Traitor, and you will be brought up on charges for Treason before a Court of the Citizens of this Country.[7]

Thompson eventually called off her march, but not before she had gained national notoriety as a self-proclaimed spokesperson for the militia movement. In the wake of the Oklahoma City bombing, she received even more media coverage.

Militia of Montana. Several militia organizations have been active in Montana, most notably the Militia of Montana (MOM), whose widely circulated literature and training programs for out-of-state activists have made it one of the most visible militias in the country. MOM is led by the brothers John and David Trochmann and David's son Randy Trochmann. John Trochmann was a strong supporter of Randy Weaver, and his family visited the Weavers with supplies before the shooting began. For some years he also cultivated ties to Aryan Nations, although in interviews with the mainstream press Trochmann has downplayed this connection.

MOM has been particularly effective in using the issue of gun control to draw in possible recruits. In strongly pro-gun Montana, MOM has attracted crowds of hundreds of people to meetings with gun control as their lead theme. Only a relatively small fraction have returned for additional meetings, in which the New World Order conspiracy is discussed and attendees are urged to organize their own small, eight- to fourteen-member militia cells to fight federal tyranny.

Some MOM leaders have also traveled for speaking engagements outside Montana. One of them, Bob Fletcher, told an audience in Denver in January 1995: "You better damn well learn how to use a gun if you don't know how to use one now. When the poop hits the fan, you will use those weapons to protect your food and your family. . . . Everyone needs to have a food supply, too. It is imperative. In terms of ammo, if you don't have bullets now, you better flat get them. . . . You are going to get flat screwed if you don't do anything."[8]

Michigan Militias and Mark Koernke. Several militia organizations have sprung up in Michigan, mostly around the issue of gun control. Michigan militia organizers have emphasized the idea that the federal government is planning to wage war against citizens who

Supporters of the Michigan Militia at Gunstock '95, a rally held by the Gun Owners of Macomb County to oppose gun-control legislation. Speakers attacked the Clinton administration, the FBI, and others that they referred to as "gun grabbers." Some suggested that the government blew up the Oklahoma City federal building to discredit the pro-gun movement.

Commander Dick Whitten at Fort Wolverine, the base and training center for the Northern Michigan Regional Militia, 1st brigade, during a training weekend. Whitten owns the land where Fort Wolverine is located.

refuse to give up their guns. "We are preparing to defend our freedom," Ray Southwell, a militia spokesman, has said. "The way things are going, I think bullets might be as valuable as gold and silver one day soon." [9]

One of the most influential national proponents of militia activism hails from Michigan—Mark Koernke. Like Linda Thompson, Koernke has sold his videos and other materials and often has spoken at militia-related events. Broadcasting on shortwave radio in the early 1990s as "Mark from Michigan," Koernke attracted many fans among militia supporters—including Timothy McVeigh.

Excerpts from
The Turner Diaries

This novel, first published in 1978, has been immensely popular among white supremacists and antigovernment extremists and is a particular favorite of Timothy McVeigh. Set in the early 1990s, it takes the form of entries in the diary of Earl Turner, a member of the "Organization," an underground group dedicated to fighting a race war to establish white people as the absolute masters of the planet. In the book, Turner is admitted to the Organization's inner circle of leadership, called the "Order."

> *October 6, 1991.* Americans have lost their right to be free. Slavery is the just and proper state for a people who have grown as soft, self-indulgent, careless, credulous, and befuddled as we have.
>
> Indeed, we are already slaves. We have allowed a diabolically clever, alien minority [Jews] to put chains on our souls and our minds. These spiritual chains are a truer mark of slavery than the iron chains which are yet to come.
>
> Why didn't we rebel 35 years ago, when they took our schools away from us and began converting them into racially mixed jungles? Why didn't we throw them all out of the country 50 years ago, instead of letting them use us as cannon fodder in their war to subjugate Europe [World War II]? . . .
>
> If the Organization fails in its task now,

everything will be lost—our history, our heritage, all the blood and sacrifices and upward striving of countless thousands of years. The Enemy we are fighting fully intends to destroy the racial basis of our existence.

No excuse for our failure will have any meaning, for there will be only a swarming horde of indifferent, mulatto zombies to hear it. There will be no White men to remember us—either to blame us for our weakness or forgive us for our folly.

The next excerpt describes an event that bears an eerie resemblance to what took place in Oklahoma City in 1995. Earl Turner and his four-person guerrilla cell are assigned the task of destroying FBI headquarters in Washington. They fuel their bomb with thousands of pounds of fertilizer and heating oil, pack it into a truck, then drive the truck into the loading area of the building, where it explodes:

October 13, 1991. At 9:15 yesterday morning our bomb went off in the FBI's national headquarters building. Our worries about the relatively small size of the bomb were unfounded; the damage is immense. . . .

We were still two blocks away when the pavement shuddered violently under our feet. An instant later the blast wave hit us—a deafening "ka-whoomp," followed by an enormous roaring, crashing sound, accentuated by the higher-pitched noise of shattering glass all around us. . . .

We ran the final two blocks. . . .

Dozens of people were scurrying around the freight entrance to the central courtyard, some going in and some coming out. Many were bleeding profusely from cuts, and all had expressions of shock or dazed disbelief on their faces. . . .

The scene in the courtyard was one of utter devastation. . . . Overturned trucks and automobiles, smashed office furniture, and building rubble were strewn wildly about— and so were the bodies of a shockingly large number of victims. . . .

All day yesterday and most of today we watched the TV coverage of rescue crews bringing the dead and injured out of the building. It is a heavy burden of responsibility for us to bear, since most of the victims of our bomb were only pawns who were no more committed to the sick philosophy or the racially destructive goals of the System than we are.

But there is no way we can destroy the System without hurting many thousands of innocent people—no way. It is a cancer too deeply rooted in our flesh. And if we don't destroy the System before it destroys us—if we don't cut this cancer out of our living flesh—our whole race will die.

The Organization purposely adopts terrorism—not only against the government but also against the general population—as a central tactic in its effort to topple the U.S. government. As the race war escalates, the Organization takes control of much of

California and establishes an all-white enclave there. Great numbers of white "traitors" are executed. Black residents are forced to leave the area, and Jews as well as light-skinned "mixed breeds" are executed so that they won't try to pass as white. After visiting a farm in the enclave, Turner remarks:

> My most profound impression comes from the fact that every face I saw in the fields was White: no Chicanos, no Orientals, no Blacks, no mongrels. The air seems cleaner, the sun brighter, life more joyous. What a wonderful difference this single accomplishment of our revolution has made!

In the end, Earl Turner dies a hero's death in a suicide mission after dropping a nuclear bomb on the Pentagon. An "Epilog" tells the story of what happens after Turner's death: Nuclear weapons as well as worldwide conventional warfare wipe out most of the world's population. The victorious remnant is entirely white. The Order rules the world.

Excerpts from The Turner Diaries *by Andrew MacDonald (a pen name for William L. Pierce), (Hillsboro, WV: National Vanguard Books, 1978).*

CHAPTER FIVE

Timothy McVeigh, Terry Nichols, and Oklahoma City

"Something big is going to happen."

Timothy McVeigh to
his friend Terry Nichols,
on April 16, 1995 [1]

Timothy James McVeigh was born on April 23, 1968, in Pendleton, New York, a suburb of Buffalo. His father, William McVeigh, worked in a nearby auto parts factory. In 1984, when Tim was in high school, his mother left home with Tim's two sisters and divorced Tim's father. Tim continued to live with his father, in a smaller house in suburban Buffalo. About this time, his father first noticed that Tim was keenly interested in guns and survivalism, stocking supplies in their cellar to be prepared in case of war or some similar upheaval.

After graduating from high school in 1986, Tim McVeigh worked at an armored car service and a sporting goods store. He and a friend teamed up to buy a plot of land to use for target-shooting.

In May 1988, McVeigh signed up for a stint in the U.S. Army. He received his basic training at Fort Benning, Georgia. Men who served with McVeigh noticed that he was intensely interested not only in weapons and survival literature but also in far-right and racist extremism. Fellow soldiers also recall that McVeigh strongly opposed gun-control legislation then being considered in Congress.

But McVeigh was, in many ways, a model soldier—disciplined, obedient, and unusually diligent in his duties. In early 1991, McVeigh was promoted to sergeant and went into combat as a tank gunner in the Gulf War, where he earned a Bronze Star.

McVeigh wanted to join the Army's elite Special Forces—the Green Berets. Right after the Gulf War, he was called back to the United States to try out for the Special Forces training program. He was concerned that, just coming off combat duty, he wasn't in good enough shape to pass the grueling tryout, and he dropped out after only two days. Afterward, he seems to have lost enthusiasm for the Army and opted for an early end to his tour of duty.

Honorably discharged from the Army while serving at Fort Riley, Kansas, at the end of 1991, McVeigh then joined the New York National Guard, which he left six months later. He lived with his father and worked as a security guard during these months. In February, he wrote a letter to the local newspaper railing against the government and closing with: "Is a civil war imminent? Do we have to shed blood to reform the current system? I hope it doesn't come to that, but it might." [2]

Around the end of 1992, Tim McVeigh packed up his belongings and moved out of his father's house. Between then and the time of the Oklahoma City bombing in April 1995, McVeigh drifted and was only intermittently employed. He is believed to have made some or most of his living buying and selling weapons and military supplies at gun shows and, using a pseudonym and a mail drop, through the mail. (In 1993, for example, using the name "T. Tuttle," McVeigh advertised military equipment for sale in the Liberty Lobby publication *The Spotlight.*)

All kinds of antigovernment extremist literature were passed around as commonly as the weapons on sale at the gun shows that McVeigh frequented, and McVeigh seems to have immersed himself in the gun culture of the new militia movement. McVeigh himself peddled copies of one particular book in addition to whatever military supplies he had on offer. The book, which fellow soldiers recall McVeigh reading when he was in the Army, was *The Turner Diaries*, the viciously racist, anti-Semitic, antigovernment novel about all-out race war. "He carried that book all the time," according to a gun collector who traveled the same gun-show circuit as McVeigh. "He sold it at the shows. He'd have a few copies in the cargo pocket of his cammies [camouflage fatigues]. . . . It was like he was looking for converts." [3] Several of the book's heroes together blow up FBI headquarters in Washington with a bomb they had made out of thousands of pounds of fertilizer and heating oil—a scenario eerily similar to what would happen at the federal building in Oklahoma City in 1995.

From mid-1993 until March 1995, McVeigh's mailing address was a private mail drop in Kingman, Arizona. For some of this time, he lived in a nearby trailer park.

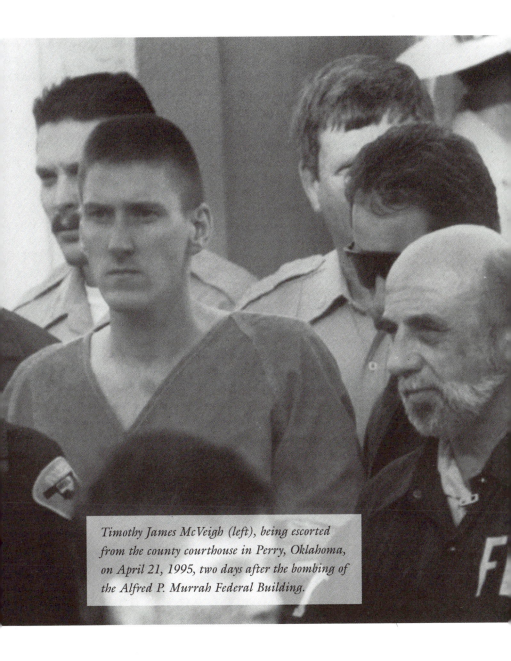

Timothy James McVeigh (left), being escorted from the county courthouse in Perry, Oklahoma, on April 21, 1995, two days after the bombing of the Alfred P. Murrah Federal Building.

He cultivated a military appearance and wore short hair and military-style clothes. He owned guns and fired them often, but this wasn't considered particularly odd in an area where target practice is a common hobby.

The sparsely populated, isolated region around Kingman, in northwestern Arizona, has been a haven for paramilitary antigovernment extremists. (An antigovernment hate group known as the Arizona Patriots was active there in the 1980s. By the time McVeigh arrived, however, the Patriots had many sympathizers but no apparent organizational structure.) McVeigh's friends in the area tended to be former military men with strong interests in guns and antigovernment ideas. One of them, Michael Fortier, had grown up there, served with McVeigh at Fort Riley, and is believed to have drawn McVeigh to the area. Fortier would later agree to testify against McVeigh when the government was building its case in the Oklahoma City bombing.

Although McVeigh spent much of his time in the two years before April 1995 in Arizona, he moved around a lot. He lived for a while at a farm in Decker, Michigan, owned by the family of one of his army buddies, Terry Nichols, and run by Terry's brother James Nichols.

Terry Lynn Nichols and his brother James grew up in rural Michigan. When their parents divorced in 1974, the brothers moved to Decker with their mother, to farm a plot of land she owned. During the widespread farming crisis of the late 1970s and 1980s, several friends and neighbors of the Nicholses went bankrupt and lost their family farms. The Nichols brothers came to see this as the fault of the federal government.

Terry was married in 1981 and moved to a nearby farm with his wife, Lana, and her two children from a previous marriage. Soon the couple had a son of their own, Joshua. The marriage foundered, and by 1988, Lana was living with another man and visiting Terry and the kids only occasionally.

At a dead end, Terry Nichols joined the Army, on exactly the same day as Tim McVeigh. The two men became close friends, even though McVeigh was thirteen years younger than Nichols. They went through basic training together at Fort Benning and were both stationed at Fort Riley.

Nichols had taken his young son to Kansas with him, and being a single parent as well as an infantryman proved to be too much for him. He was granted a hardship discharge in May 1989, before McVeigh was sent to fight in the Gulf War. Terry returned to his brother's farm.

Later that year, he traveled to the Philippines in search of a bride and married a teenager named Marife in her hometown of Cebu. By the time Nichols arranged for Marife's immigration and she joined him in Michigan, Marife was pregnant by a former boyfriend. Terry agreed to raise her baby boy as his own, and in 1992 the couple also had a baby girl.

Through all this time, Terry Nichols, his brother, and Tim McVeigh remained close. McVeigh lived and worked from time to time at the Nichols farm. The three men shared extreme antigovernment views, which seem to have intensified after the federal siege of the Branch Davidian cult's compound near Waco, Texas. In early 1993, McVeigh traveled to Waco and was photographed among the spectators during the fifty-one-day standoff there. In April he and the Nichols brothers watched the fiery conclusion to the siege on television at the Nichols farm. Later, McVeigh visited the site again. McVeigh, even more than the Nichols brothers, appears to have been deeply upset by what happened at Waco, and often voiced rage about the government's conduct there.

Terry Nichols, though more soft-spoken than his brother, landed in court several times in Michigan as a result of his attempts to cut all his ties with government. Having apparently been strongly influenced by "patriot movement" ideas similar to those of the Posse Comitatus, he refused to recognize the authority of most government. In one legal dispute, he filed court papers asserting that he was "no longer one of your citizens of your de facto government. [I am a] nonresident alien, nonforeigner. Stranger." [4]

McVeigh, and the Nichols brothers to some extent, became involved with the locally active Michigan Militia, and literature of that group was found at the farm after the Oklahoma City bombing. Although the three attended at least some militia meetings, militia leaders have denied that any one of them was a member and claim to have thrown two of the three out of one meeting in early 1995.

The three also seem to have become involved with the shadowy Michigan Militia-at-Large, a heavily armed and secretive contingent of extremists too radical for even the Michigan Militia. A well-known spokesman for this radical fringe was Mark Koernke ("Mark from Michigan"), a janitor living in Dexter, near the Nichols farm. Timothy McVeigh was a fan of Koernke's daily short-wave radio program (which was pulled off the air after the Oklahoma City bombing). McVeigh may even have served as a contact person for Koernke and as a bodyguard for him at gun shows where Koernke was a featured speaker. Koernke has denied knowing McVeigh.

Neighbors noticed that McVeigh and the Nichols brothers seemed unusually interested in guns and other weapons, including explosives. Terry Nichols seems to have collaborated with McVeigh in the business of buying and selling weapons and army surplus material at gun shows. The two brothers and McVeigh occasionally made and set off small bombs at the farm.

After the accidental death of Marife's two-year-old son Jason in November 1993, Nichols and his wife left Michigan. Nichols worked as a ranch hand in Kansas during the summer of 1994.

Tim McVeigh visited Terry Nichols at the ranch in September, and soon afterward Terry packed up and left. Within the next month, according to officials investigating the Oklahoma City bombing, Nichols and McVeigh used aliases to rent several storage sheds in Kansas, purchased two tons of fertilizer, and stole explosives supplies from a Kansas quarry.

Also according to investigators, sometime in late 1994, McVeigh and Nichols suddenly seemed to have a lot more cash, perhaps from a robbery of a gun dealer. (They have been linked to some of the guns from this robbery but are not believed to have commited the robbery themselves.) Terry Nichols's ex-wife Lana has said that in mid-December she opened one of his storage sheds and found gold bullion and cash.

Also in mid-December, Tim McVeigh paid a visit to

Oklahoma City with Michael Fortier. Fortier later told investigators that McVeigh showed him the Alfred P. Murrah Federal Building.

In January 1995, Terry Nichols bought a small house for himself, Marife, and their daughter, in Herington, Kansas, about 270 miles (435 kilometers) north of Oklahoma City. According to Lana, he had had a falling out with Tim McVeigh and was trying to start a new life.

McVeigh was in Arizona in February 1995, and he visited the Nichols farm in Michigan in March.

On April 3, Terry Nichols rented a U-Haul trailer that investigators later suspected might have been used to carry bomb ingredients to one of the several rented storage sheds near Nichols's home.

After another stay in Arizona, McVeigh returned to Kansas. From April 14 to 18, he stayed at the Dreamland Motel in Junction City, Kansas, about 30 miles (48 kilometers) from Nichols's home.

On the evening of April 15, someone in McVeigh's room at the motel ordered delivery of Chinese food using the name Bob Kling. The deliveryman later said that the person who accepted delivery at the room didn't look like either McVeigh or Nichols, nor did he look like the man that investigators, after the bombing, dubbed "John Doe No. 2."

On April 16, at about 3 P.M., McVeigh called Nichols from Oklahoma City and asked him for a ride back to Kansas. (Investigators later speculated that McVeigh left his own car in Oklahoma City to serve as a getaway vehicle after the bombing.) Nichols later told investigators that he picked up McVeigh hours later near the Alfred P. Murrah Federal Building. While they were on the road heading back to Kansas, Nichols has said, McVeigh told him that "something big is going to happen." Nichols dropped McVeigh in Junction City after midnight.

The following afternoon, in Junction City, McVeigh rented a previously reserved yellow Ryder truck using an alias (Bob Kling) and a fake driver's license with an April 19 birth date—the day of the fire at Waco. He was accompanied by another man, "John Doe No. 2." McVeigh parked the truck in the Dreamland Motel parking lot.

The next morning, April 18, a Ryder truck like the one McVeigh rented was seen parked at a lake near Nichols's home in Herington, next to a pickup truck similar to one owned by Terry Nichols. Prosecutors in the Oklahoma City bombing case would later allege that this was where McVeigh and Nichols actually assembled the Oklahoma City bomb, inside the truck.

Nichols, however, has told investigators a different story: That morning, McVeigh borrowed Nichols's pickup truck for more than six hours, then drove Nichols to one of the rented storage sheds and told him: "If I don't come back in a while, you clean out the shed."[5] (Nichols cleaned out the shed on April 20, the day after the bombing.)

On April 19—the second anniversary of the fire at Waco—shortly before 9 A.M., several witnesses have said that they saw Timothy McVeigh near the Alfred P. Murrah Federal Building in Oklahoma City. The rented Ryder truck, packed with thousands of pounds of explosives, arrived at about 8:45 or 8:50 A.M. At 9:02 A.M., it exploded.

While rescuers swarmed over the bomb site seeking survivors, investigators also examined the rubble, looking for clues. It was immediately obvious that the explosion had been no accident. It had been caused, they soon determined, by a simple but powerful bomb made mostly of commonly available ammonium nitrate fertilizer and fuel oil. It was also obvious that the huge blast must have required hundreds, perhaps thousands, of pounds of explosives, brought to the building in a car or truck.

Early on, many people assumed that the bomb had been planted by Middle Eastern terrorists, like the bomb set off at the World Trade Center in New York in 1993. National news media reported that investigators were seeking several Arab men for questioning. Muslim mosques across the country reported threats and harassment, apparently in retaliation for the bombing.

Within one day, however, the investigation focused on two suspects not linked to Middle Eastern terrorism. In a lucky break, investigators had found a vehicle identification number stamped on a piece of wreckage that they believed came from the vehicle that had contained the bomb. They traced the number to the Ryder rental agency in Junction City, where they found that it belonged to a truck rented by two white men, believed to be in their twenties, who used false identification, looked like they might be soldiers from nearby Fort Riley, and spoke without foreign accents. Working with employees at the rental agency, the FBI was able to create two sketches of the suspects—John Doe No. 1 and John Doe No. 2— which soon circulated all over the United States.

About an hour and a half after the bombing, Timothy McVeigh was stopped for a traffic violation in Perry, Oklahoma. He was carrying a loaded semiautomatic handgun in a shoulder holster at the time and was arrested on weapons charges. McVeigh listed James Nichols as his next of kin, using the Michigan farm address. His bond hearing was delayed for a day because the judge's schedule was full.

Meanwhile, bombing investigators turned up McVeigh's name from records at the Dreamland Motel and from a lead phoned in by a former coworker who recognized McVeigh in the police sketch and description of "John Doe No. 1."

On the morning of April 21, the local police handed over a politely silent, stone-faced McVeigh to federal authorities for questioning in connection with the bombing. Residue from bomb ingredients was later found on his clothes and in his car, which also contained antigovernment pamphlets about Waco.

While in federal custody, McVeigh allegedly called himself a "prisoner of war" and refused to answer questions. At a court hearing on April 27, at which McVeigh was denied bail, the federal judge presiding announced: "The court finds an indelible trail of evidence that starts in Junction City and ends up at the front door of the Murrah building." [6] By then, federal investigators had pieced together McVeigh's movements in the days leading up to the event and had become convinced that they had sufficient evidence to prosecute him as, at the very least, a co-conspirator in the bombing, and possibly as its mastermind.

Hours after McVeigh's arrest was announced, on April 21, Terry Nichols turned himself in for questioning. (In Michigan, James Nichols was arrested and held for several weeks, then released and not charged in the bomb-

Terry Nichols, outside the courthouse in Wichita, Kansas, on May 10, 1995, after being charged in connection with the Oklahoma City bombing.

ing.) At first, investigators thought that Terry Nichols might be "John Doe No. 2," but he didn't look like the apparently much younger man who accompanied McVeigh to the Ryder agency. The identity of John Doe No. 2 remained a mystery.

A search of Terry Nichols's home in Herington turned up antigovernment pamphlets, assault weapons, several empty fertilizer drums, and some parts used to ignite explosives. Also found was a receipt for the purchase of a ton of fertilizer by someone who was using the name "Mike Havens," dated September 1994, with one of Timothy McVeigh's fingerprints on it. "Mike Havens" purchased another ton of fertilizer from the same source in October.

On May 10, Terry Nichols was formally charged with participating in the Oklahoma City bombing. At the time he was charged, investigators said that Nichols had admitted driving the rental truck suspected of carrying the bomb to Oklahoma City, but had maintained that he didn't have anything to do with the explosion.

In December 1995, in an effort to ensure a fair trial, a new judge, Richard P. Matsch, was appointed to try the bombing case. (He replaced a judge whose ability to be fair was questioned because his offices had been damaged by the blast.) In February 1996, Judge Matsch ruled that the trial should be held in Denver, Colorado, rather than in Oklahoma, where an impartial jury would be particularly difficult to assemble because so many people's lives there had been touched by the bombing.

If convicted, both McVeigh and Nichols could face the death penalty. Both have pleaded not guilty.

CHAPTER SIX

After the Bombing

"It is grotesque to suggest that anybody in this country who raises legitimate questions about the size and scope of the federal government has any implication in this."

> House Speaker Newt Gingrich, reacting to suggestions that his verbal attacks on government bureaucrats might have helped create a climate fostering the Oklahoma City bombing [1]

Across the United States, the overwhelming reaction to the Oklahoma City bombing was outrage. President Clinton called it "an attack on innocent children and defenseless citizens. It was an act of cowardice, and it was evil." [2] Attorney General Janet Reno said that the federal government would seek the death penalty against the person or persons responsible.

The arrest of Timothy McVeigh and the Nichols brothers focused national attention on the militia movement and the climate of hatred that had encouraged it. Immediately, much of the wide section of mainstream America that had knowingly or indirectly supported or sympathized with the militia movement began to turn against it.

THE POLITICIANS RESPOND

Politicians, mostly conservative Republicans, who previously had whipped up voter support with strongly worded attacks on government bureaucrats began to backpedal. Some sought to distance themselves from the antigovernment extremist fringe; others expressed outrage that anyone might think that their strident rhetoric had anything to do with antigovernment violence. Legislation favored by militia supporters suddenly became much more controversial: Congressional Republicans decided to postpone the vote they earlier had promised pro-gun lobbyists on repealing the assault weapons ban passed by the Democrat-controlled Congress in 1994.

Individual members of Congress who previously had accepted or encouraged militia support were called to account. When the office of Republican Representative Helen Chenoweth of Idaho was asked after the bombing about how it was that the Militia of Montana was using a videotape of one of her fund-raising speeches, a spokeswoman insisted that the tape was being sold without permission. [3] Similarly, before the bombing, militia-friendly Republican Representative Steve Stockman of Texas had written an article for *Guns & Ammo* magazine contending that the federal government had deliberately provoked confrontation at the Branch Davidian compound in Waco in order to drum up support for its ban on assault weapons. When the article was published, less than a month after Oklahoma City, Stockman insisted that he hadn't meant that the Clinton administration had actually wanted people to get killed at Waco, and noted that the article "came out at a poor time." [4]

After Oklahoma City, the National Rifle Association was sharply and widely criticized for its incendiary rhetoric about "jack-booted Government thugs." Many observers asserted that this sort of language encouraged antigovernment violence. Former president and lifetime NRA member George Bush publicly resigned his membership in protest. "Your broadside against federal agents deeply offends my own sense of decency and honor, and it offends my concept of service to country," he wrote in his resignation letter. "It indirectly slurs a wide array of government law enforcement officials, who are out there, day and night, laying their lives on the line for all of us." [5]

Pat Buchanan's 1995–1996 presidential campaign offered an ongoing reflection of changing attitudes toward the extremist fringe. From its beginning, before the Oklahoma City bombing, Buchanan's campaign had drawn significant support from the large number of disaffected Americans drifting near the mouth of the funnel from mainstream to extreme, as well as from Christian Identity and white supremacist extremists deep within the funnel. In several Southern states, for example, Buchanan was aided by the campaign apparatus developed there by and for the former Klansman and neo-Nazi politician David Duke.

As his campaign wore on, however, Buchanan came under increasing pressure to repudiate his ties to the extremist fringe. Eventually, his campaign removed several extremists from leadership positions—most notably Gun

Owners of America's Larry Pratt, who had shared the speaker's podium with an extensive assortment of white supremacists at various rallies and other gatherings, including the conference held in Estes Park, Colorado, after Ruby Ridge. Buchanan reluctantly ousted Pratt as his campaign cochairman in February 1996. Even afterward, Buchanan's often racially loaded rhetoric continued to pander to the extremist fringe: "When I raise my hand to take that oath of office your New World Order comes crashing down," he said at a rally later that month. [6]

Extremists got the message. Such unabashedly bigoted organizations as Christian Identity Online and the "white racialist" information clearinghouse Stormfront featured the Buchanan campaign on their World Wide Web sites and referred prospective volunteers to the campaign's own Web site.

But perhaps mainstream voters got the message, too, and were turned off by it. For whatever reasons, Buchanan's campaign lost momentum not long after the Pratt dismissal. He never received more than 30 percent of the vote in any of the Republican primaries.

THE GOVERNMENT RESPONDS

At the time of the Oklahoma City bombing, most states already had some laws in effect restricting or regulating paramilitary groups, but these laws were rarely enforced. Some of the laws were quite old, dating from the period of Ku Klux Klan terrorism in the South just after the Civil War. After Oklahoma City, law-enforcement officials across the country pondered how and in what circumstances they should bring legal action against militias. Respect for the constitutional rights of militia members to free association, assembly, and speech limit what law enforcement can do about their activities. As one law professor put it: "There is no law against grown men dressing up in camouflage uniforms and playing soldier with legally acquired weapons."[7]

But there are laws against terrorism, and immediately after the Oklahoma City bombing President Clinton proposed beefing them up. "We're going to have to be very tough in dealing with this," he said several days after the bombing, and asked Congress to pass legislation giving the government new powers and more money to combat terrorism.[8] (Several days of Congressional hearings about the militias had been held shortly before the Oklahoma City bombing, attracting little attention at the time.)

The Senate passed its version of the antiterrorism legislation in June, but a similar measure stalled in the House of Representatives. A peculiar alliance of liberal Democrats and conservative Republicans objected to parts of the legislation that they said would allow the federal government to violate the freedoms of individual citizens. At the end of 1995, work on the bill was put off until the next year's session of Congress.

Meanwhile, in the summer and fall after the bombing, Congress also looked into two matters of great concern to militia members: Waco and Ruby Ridge. Hearings were held in both the House and the Senate, and federal law-enforcement officials detailed changes that had been made at their agencies to prevent such deadly outcomes from recurring in the future. Although the Senate issued a report harshly critical of federal agencies involved in the deaths at Ruby Ridge, no legislative action was proposed.

In April 1996, just in time for the first anniversary of the Oklahoma City bombing, Congress passed and President Clinton signed into law a final version of the antiterrorism legislation crafted in response to the bombing. The major provisions of the bill included:

- Allotment of up to $1 billion over four years for the federal government to spend fighting terrorism;
- Requirement that criminals in many federal cases make restitution to their victims;
- More power for the federal government to exclude or deport foreigners suspected of ties to terrorists or convicted of other crimes;
- More power for the federal government to prosecute U.S. citizens who raise money for groups that participate in terrorism, even if the money is used for legal activities;
- Requirement that manufacturers of plastic explosives (but not the fertilizer used in the Oklahoma City bombing) mix microscopic "taggants" into their products so they can be traced;
- Establishment of sharp limits on "habeas corpus" rights, limiting the ability of prisoners, especially those on death row, to appeal their convictions or sentences to higher courts.

Civil liberties activists strongly objected to the legislation, claiming that it would seriously erode the free-speech and free-association rights of U.S. citizens. Furthermore, they said, while it would have little effect on determined terrorists, it would have a disastrous effect on innocent prisoners wrongly incarcerated for unrelated crimes, as it would strictly limit their access to the courts.

In an unusually swift move, the U.S. Supreme Court agreed just days after the legislation became law to review whether several of its provisions were permitted by the U.S. Constitution. In June, the court unanimously affirmed that one of the law's provisions on federal court appeals by state prisoners was permitted. But other legal issues raised by the antiterrorism legislation remained unresolved. Several additional provisions of the law slowly made their way through the lower courts to an expected Supreme Court review. Congress considered even more antiterrorism legislation in response to the July 1996 explosions aboard TWA Flight 800 off Long Island, New York, and at a park near Olympic Games venues in Atlanta, Georgia.

THE MILITIAS' RESPONSE

Reaction to the Oklahoma City bombing among militia supporters was mixed. Most unequivocally condemned it. Some, however, asserted that if the federal government had punished the agents who burned down the Branch Davidian compound at Waco, then the Oklahoma City bombing would never have happened.

Others were convinced that the federal government itself had blown up the federal building. "Those who know and study history can reasonably assume the government was behind the Oklahoma City bombing," Louis Beam asserted.[9] Another antigovernment extremist wrote: "I accuse the federal government of planning and perpetrating the most horrible crimes, a series which culminated in the April 19, 1995, bombing of the federal building in Oklahoma City. This was a deliberate conspiracy by corrupt and treasonous elements in the

federal agencies in Washington as part of a plan to provoke martial law, confiscate legal guns from American
citizens, and to wipe out the citizens militia of the several states."[10]

The bombing focused an intense media spotlight on
the previously shadowy militia movement and threw parts
of it into disarray. Ray Southwell and another Michigan
militia leader were suspended from their duties after publicly accusing the Japanese government of perpetrating
the bombing. Mark Koernke's radio show was pulled off
the air. A group calling itself the Oregon Militia disbanded,
and other previously aggressive militia groups became
quieter and less inflammatory. Many militia members
questioned whether they should continue their militia in-
volvement. Communities that were once militia-friendly
became less tolerant and more vigilant after bombing
suspects McVeigh and Nichols were linked to the militia
movement. Militia supporters became fewer and more
isolated.

But a radical, potentially violent hard core remained,
with some membes of it organized into underground
"leaderless resistance" cells. "If one thing has been dem-
onstrated in Oklahoma," a Christian Identity minister
wrote, "it is that the people can strike back at ZOG [Zi-
onist Occupational Government] with or without 'assault
weapons.' Our treasonous politicians would do well to
ponder their fate at the hands of angry and determined
people who they are even now planning to oppress with
more unconstitutional legislation."[11]

Since Oklahoma City, the leaders of hate groups have
continued to encourage these "angry and determined
people" to move deeper into the funnel. William Pierce,

author of *The Turner Diaries,* wrote for a radio broadcast soon after the bombing:

> I listened to the expressions of pious outrage by
> Bill Clinton and Janet Reno and the other gov-
> ernment gangsters on television that evening, and
> I thought, "You hypocrites! What do you expect?
> You are the real terrorists. When a government
> engages in terrorism against its own citizens, it
> should not be surprised when some of those citi-
> zens strike back and engage in terrorism against
> the government. You are the ones responsible for
> this bombing, for the deaths of these children.". . .
>   It's not just the Waco massacre . . . which
> makes so many Americans hate their government.
> It's what the government has done to America.

Pierce offered a list of "destructive" things that the government had done to America: "flooding . . . our country with non-Whites from the Third World" and from
Mexico; "catering to the worst elements in the population, buying their votes with welfare"; taxing oppressively
and enacting unreasonably restrictive laws (particularly
gun control); "turning away from the people who built
America"; and "cynically [promoting] 'multiculturalism,'
with the consequent ruin of our schools, the degradation
of our popular culture, and the conversion of our cities
into crime-infested hell holes." He asserted:

> The government and the controlled [Jewish] me-
> dia are responsible for the spiritual poisoning of
> our young people: young Whites singing rap dit-
> ties and behaving like Blacks. . . .

The privileged classes . . . —the Jews and the politicians and the homosexuals and the minorities and the female executives—who believe that this is the best of all possible worlds, have no idea how angry, how furious, normal Americans are.

When people are pushed as far as they are willing to go, and when they believe that they have nothing left to lose, then they will resort to terrorism. There will be more and more such people in the future. Even if they have no well thought-out plan, even if they belong to no organization and have no real ideology, even if they are only striking out as angry, frustrated individuals, their numbers and their deeds will grow. [12]

Some of these "angry, frustrated individuals" did in fact commit acts of violence in the months after Oklahoma City, but on a much smaller scale than the federal building bombing:

- In July 1995, a Texas man was arrested for plotting to blow up the large Internal Revenue Service (IRS) installation in Austin, which employs more than 4,000 federal workers. (Several people said that the man had told them he planned to blow up federal sites across the country.)
- In October, antigovernment notes referring to Waco and Ruby Ridge were found near the scene of a passenger train derailment in Arizona caused by sabotage. One person was killed, and about a hundred others were injured.
- In April 1996, Christian Identity adherents were believed to be responsible for several pipe bombs set off

in Spokane, Washington, including one at Spokane City Hall. No one was injured.

- Also in April, federal agents arrested two militia members in Georgia who had acquired bomb materials and allegedly were fashioning them into pipe bombs.

THE FREEMEN AND THE VIPER MILITIA

The best-known militia-related incident in the year or so after Oklahoma City were the Freemen standoff in remote rural Montana and the arrest of the Viper Militia in suburban Arizona.

The Freemen story began in the late 1970s and early 1980s, long before the Oklahoma City bombing. Montana farmer Ralph E. Clark and his family and ranching partners borrowed large sums of money when credit was easy. They couldn't pay it back, even while receiving more than a half-million dollars in federal farming subsidies. Clark and his associates teamed up with assorted antigovernment activists and tax protesters from outside the area. In 1995 they holed up at the 960-acre (389-hectare) Clark homestead (the government had already foreclosed on the ranch to pay Clark's debts). They renamed the homestead Justus Township, and set up a "common-law" government there. Strongly influenced by Christian Identity and Posse Comitatus thinking, the self-named Freemen refused to recognize the authority of any government but their own.

Many of the Freemen issued arrest and death warrants for various government officials and wrote millions of dollars worth of bogus checks. They also taught other antigovernment extremists to follow in their footsteps by offering seminars at the ranch on tax evasion and finan-

Freeman Dave Sullivan of Bozeman, Montana, working in support of the Freemen holed up for months on Justus Township.

cial fraud.) The Freemen allegedly defrauded dozens of victims of nearly two million dollars, before federal agents moved in to stop them.

Mindful of the bloody outcomes of the standoffs at Waco and Ruby Ridge, the federal agencies responsible for bringing the heavily armed Freemen to justice took a patient, low-key approach. For months, they simply watched and waited. Then, in March 1996, they lured two Freemen leaders away from their living quarters and arrested them.

The federal agents didn't provoke a confrontation. Instead, they stayed mostly out of sight, monitored phone calls and radio signals from the ranch, and allowed outside family members and third-party negotiators (including, in April, Bo Gritz and Jack McLamb) access to the Freemen, in the hope that everyone at the ranch could be persuaded to come out without violence.

Finally their patience paid off. "I am pleased to announce that today we accomplished our mission," FBI Director Louis Freeh told reporters on June 13, 1996. "Everyone has left the Freemen-occupied ranch, and those wanted on criminal charges have been taken into custody." Not a shot had been fired; everyone left the ranch safely.

Freeh emphasized that "to achieve this peaceful resolution the FBI acted absolutely honorably in all of the negotiations. We made no deals to drop or lessen the federal charges against anyone. Our posture from the very beginning was to build solid federal criminal cases and arrest everyone charged with a federal crime whenever we could do so safely. We never wavered from that position."

Freeh also noted that the Freemen standoff had been resolved using new FBI procedures, intended to prevent such deadly outcomes as those at Ruby Ridge and Waco. "I am gratified that both the new procedures and FBI employees performed as I had expected they would," Freeh said. "I think the American people can take great comfort in the fact the law was enforced, as it should always be, and that it was done in a way that did not bring harm to anyone." [13]

In contrast to the months-long Freemen standoff, law-enforcement action against the Viper Militia was swift and sudden. Just before 8 A.M. on July 1, in a carefully coordinated action, federal and local agents arrested ten men and two women in the suburbs of Phoenix, Arizona, and charged them with weapons offenses and with conspiring to blow up several federal buildings as well as the building housing the Phoenix police department. (All pleaded not guilty.) The twelve were believed to be the members of the secretive, little-known Viper Militia.

In the days following the arrests, a picture of the Viper Militia's activities emerged. Federal agents seized more than a hundred guns (some of them illegal automatic weapons) as well as thousands of rounds of ammunition and hundreds of pounds of explosive materials at the homes of those arrested. Videotapes and audiotapes made by the militia documented members training in the use of illegal weapons and explosives, and discussing possible federal targets. An undercover agent who had infiltrated the group at the end of 1995 said that he had been required to swear that he would seek revenge against any federal agent who took action against the group.

Although Oklahoma City bombing suspect Timothy McVeigh spent a lot of time in Arizona and associated with militia sympathizers there, he was believed to have had nothing to do with any members of the Viper Militia. The Vipers, it seems, were an independent terrorist cell. They socialized with more-mainstream gun enthusiasts and steeped themselves in widely available militia-related literature, but their illegal activities were planned and practiced in secret, independent of any outside command or control. Self-consciously or not, they were a "phantom cell" acting out Louis Beam's model of leaderless resistance.

It is impossible to know how many such cells might be in operation across the United States, or the extent of their threat. "It's a dangerous situation, and we should just not brush it off like it's not a serious situation," a member of a task force on the militia movement said after the Viper arrests. "I think law enforcement has finally gotten the message. But I'm not sure everybody else has."[14]

EPILOGUE
April 19, 1996

"People tell me, 'Take Rick's picture down, don't turn it into a shrine.' But that's what I have. I have a picture."

Tina Tomlin, one year after
the Oklahoma City bombing,
which killed her husband [1]

One year after the Oklahoma City bombing, early in the morning of April 19, 1996, thousands of people gathered at the empty place where the Alfred P. Murrah Federal Building used to be. The rubble had long since been cleared away from the site. Grass had grown. The sun was shining, and it was a fine spring day, but the mood of the crowd was somber. At exactly 9:02 A.M. they stood together for 168 seconds of silence—one second for each of the people who died in the bombing.

Later that morning, Vice President Al Gore spoke at a memorial service in Oklahoma City attended by relatives of those who died, rescue workers, and other people

President Clinton and Hillary Rodham Clinton at a memorial service held one year after the Oklahoma City bombing. President Clinton holds the hand of Jason Smith, whose mother's body was never found in the rubble of the Alfred P. Murrah Federal Building.

whose lives had been directly touched by the bombing. "Let there be no mistake," he said. "One year is a very short time. In the human heart it can be the blink of an eye. The people of Oklahoma City are mourning still. I can feel that the icy cloud of grief has lifted some since . . . last spring. But it has not disappeared, and it will never leave for good."

That anniversary morning wasn't only about sadness, though. It was also about community, strength, and hope. "Your resoluteness," the vice president continued, "has taught the world something about the state of our union: In America, terror will not triumph. Let me say it again: Terror will not triumph." [2]

NOTES

PROLOGUE
The information in this prologue came from contemporary news reports, chiefly those in the *Washington Post* and *New York Times.* Direct quotations are cited below.

1. *New York Times,* April 20, 1995.
2. *Washington Post,* April 20, 1995.
3. *Washington Post,* April 24, 1995.

CHAPTER ONE
The chief sources for this chapter are: Klanwatch/Southern Poverty Law Center's *The Ku Klux Klan: A History of Racism and Violence,* 4th edition (Montgomery, Ala.: SPLC, 1991) and *Hate, Violence, and White Supremacy: A Decade Review, 1980-1990* (Montgomery, Ala.: SPLC, December 1989), Anti-Defamation League's *Special Report: Paranoia as Patriotism: Far-Right Influences on the Militia Movement* (New York: ADL, 1995), and various hate activists' World Wide Web sites. Direct quotations are cited below.

1. David Lane, "An Open Letter to Timothy McVeigh," linked to "Independent White Racialist Homepage," a World Wide Web site, downloaded April 1996; numerous Internet postings featuring "Fourteen Words!"

2. "Statement of Faith," linked to "Christian Identity Online," a World Wide Web site, downloaded April 1996.
3. James Ellison, 1982, quoted in Klanwatch/Southern Poverty Law Center's *Hate, Violence, and White Supremacy*, p. 3.
4. For more information, see Richard Hofstadter's essay "The Paranoid Style in American Politics," in *The Paranoid Style in American Politics and Other Essays* (New York: Alfred A. Knopf, 1965).
5. "What Is the National Alliance? National Alliance Goals," from National Alliance's World Wide Web site, downloaded April 1996.
6. Ibid.
7. Two separate sources told this to the cable television channel CNN, according to Morris Dees with James Corcoran's *Gathering Storm: America's Militia Threat* (New York: HarperCollins, 1996), p. 163.
8. Anti-Defamation League's *Special Report: Paranoia as Patriotism*, p. 33.

CHAPTER TWO
1. Quoted in Kenneth S. Stern's *A Force Upon the Plain: The American Militia Movement and the Politics of Hate* (New York: Simon and Schuster, 1996), p. 108.
2. Quoted in Stern's *A Force Upon the Plain*, p. 222.
3. Ibid.
4. Chip Berlet, interviewed by David Barsamian in "Militias & Conspiracy Theories," *Z Magazine* (September 1995), p. 35.
5. Quoted in Stern's *A Force Upon the Plain*, p. 102.
6. *Washington Post*, April 25, 1995.
7. Document reproduced as Appendix 103 of "Militias: A Growing Danger: An American Jewish Committee Background Report," by Kenneth S. Stern, a brief report with about 600 pages of militia-related documents attached, released in 1995 shortly before the Oklahoma City bombing.
8. *New York Times*, April 30, 1995.

9. "Text of a recorded message made available by Tom Metzger's White Aryan Resistance," quoted in James Ridgeway's *Blood in the Face: The Ku Klux Klan, Aryan Nations, Nazi Skinheads, and the Rise of a New White Culture* (New York: Thunder's Mouth Press, 1990), p. 172.
10. Robertson, *The New World Order*, pp. 6, 37, 92, 96, 133-134, 176, 231.
11. Transcript of Pat Buchanan's 1992 speech to the Republican National Convention, linked to "The Pat Buchanan for President Link," a World Wide Web site, downloaded April 1996.

CHAPTER THREE
This chapter is derived mostly from contemporary news reports on Ruby Ridge, Waco, the Brady bill, and the assault rifle ban, chiefly from the *New York Times, Washington Post,* and *Facts on File.* Sources for direct quotations are identified below.

1. *New York Times,* Aug. 30, 1992.
2. *New York Times,* Aug. 26, 1992.
3. Jess Walter, *Every Knee Shall Bow: The Truth and Tragedy of Ruby Ridge and the Randy Weaver Family* (New York: Regan Books/HarperCollins, 1995), p. 228.
4. *New York Times,* Sept. 1, 1992.
5. "Larry King Live," April 19, 1993, quoted in *Facts on File,* April 22, 1993.
6. "Interview: Kirk Lyons of CAUSE Foundation," originally published in *Stormfront* magazine (January 1994), downloaded April 1996 from page linked to Stormfront's World Wide Web site. "CAUSE" stands for "Canada, Australia, United States, South Africa, and Europe"—parts of the world where white people have dominated.
7. "Jeff Cooper's Commentaries," dated July 16, 1993, quoted in *New York Times,* May 8, 1995.

8. Quoted in Dees, *Gathering Storm*, p. 77.
9. NRA fund-raising letter signed by Wayne R. LaPierre, Jr., dated April 13, 1995, quoted in *New York Times*, May 8, 1995.

CHAPTER FOUR
1. Quoted in *New York Times*, April 23, 1995.
2. Quoted in Dees, *Gathering Storm*, p. 1.
3. Louis R. Beam, Jr., "Leaderless Resistance," originally published in his quarterly publication *The Seditionist* (February 1992), downloaded April 1996 from World Wide Web archives linked to "Independent White Racialist Home Page."
4. Quoted in Stern's *A Force Upon the Plain*, p. 166.
5. Quoted in Stern's *A Force Upon the Plain*, p. 170.
6. Quoted in Stern's *A Force Upon the Plain*, p. 171.
7. Document reproduced as Appendix 102 of "Militias: A Growing Danger."
8. Quoted in *Denver Post*, January 22, 1995, reproduced as Appendix 71 of "Militias: A Growing Danger."
9. Quoted in *New York Times*, Nov. 14, 1994, reproduced as Appendix 46 of "Militias: A Growing Danger."

CHAPTER FIVE
Almost all of the information in this chapter is from news reports published shortly after the Oklahoma City bombing (mostly the *New York Times, Washington Post,* and a very useful Timothy McVeigh timeline in the April 30, 1995, *Buffalo News*) and from an ABC News special report broadcast on April 12, 1996: "Peter Jennings Reporting: Rage and Betrayal: The Lives of Tim McVeigh and Terry Nichols." Sources for direct quotations are cited below.

1. *Washington Post*, April 27, 1995.
2. *Washington Post*, April 27, 1995.
3. *New York Times*, July 5, 1995.
4. *Washington Post*, April 30, 1995.

5. *Washington Post,* April 30, 1995.
6. *Washington Post,* April 28, 1995.

CHAPTER SIX

This chapter is derived mostly from contemporary news reports, chiefly from the *New York Times* and the *Washington Post,* and from various hate activists' World Wide Web sites.

1. *Washington Post,* April 23, 1995.
2. *New York Times,* April 20, 1995.
3. *New York Times,* May 2, 1995.
4. *Washington Post,* May 13, 1995.
5. *Washington Post,* May 11, 1995.
6. *New York Times,* Feb. 25, 1996.
7. *New York Times,* May 10, 1995.
8. *Washington Post,* April 24, 1995.
9. Quoted in Dees, *Gathering Storm,* p. 175.
10. Eustace Mullins, "Oklahoma City—*J'Accuse!*" downloaded April 1996 from archives at Stormfront's World Wide Web site.
11. Mark Thomas, "Requiem for a Witch-Doctor," downloaded April 1996 from "The Watchman," a World Wide Web site published by the Pennsylvania Christian Posse Comitatus and the Church of Jesus Christ Christian, Aryan Nations.
12. William L. Pierce, "OKC Bombing and America's Future," identified as text from an April 29, 1995, radio broadcast, downloaded April 1996 from archives at Stormfront's World Wide Web site.
13. "June 13, 1996, statement of FBI Director Louis J. Freeh," linked to the FBI's World Wide Web home page, downloaded June 17, 1996.
14. Richard Romley, interviewed on "NewsHour with Jim Lehrer," July 5, 1996.

EPILOGUE

1. *New York Times,* April 19, 1996.
2. "NewsHour with Jim Lehrer," April 19, 1996.

FURTHER READING

Morris Dees with James Corcoran. *Gathering Storm: America's Militia Threat.* New York: HarperCollins, 1996.

James Ridgeway. *Blood in the Face: The Ku Klux Klan, Aryan Nations, Nazi Skinheads, and the Rise of a New White Culture.* New York: Thunder's Mouth Press, 1990.

Kenneth S. Stern. *A Force Upon the Plain: The American Militia Movement and the Politics of Hate.* New York: Simon and Schuster, 1996.

Tides Foundation. *Requiem for the Heartland: The Oklahoma City Bombing.* San Francisco: CollinsPublishers San Francisco, 1995.

Ken Toole. *What to Do When the Militia Comes to Town.* New York: American Jewish Committee, 1995.

Jess Walter. *Every Knee Shall Bow: The Truth and Tragedy of Ruby Ridge and the Randy Weaver Family.* New York: Regan Books/HarperCollins, 1995.

INDEX

Page numbers in *italics* refer to illustrations.